In this the love of God was manifested toward us,
that God has sent His only begotten Son into the world,
that we might live through Him.
1 John 4:9

For He made Him who knew no sin
to be sin for us,
that we might become the righteousness of God in Him.
2 Corinthians 5:21

In praise of *The Jesus Exchange*

"Many Christians, in some raw and honest place in their hearts, long for more in their relationship with God, asking, often silently: Is there something else? Is there more to being a Christian than being forgiven? Am I more than a pardoned sinner? Is there more to experience of Christ directly?

If you long for a faith that offers much more than a ticket to heaven—a faith walk that moves beyond religion and into the realm of intimate relationship with Jesus, you'll be enthralled by *The Jesus Exchange*.

Through his years of clinical practice, Dr. Bill Day has discovered that authentic healing comes not through wooden, mental assent to Christian doctrines but through fluid, spiritual attachment to God Himself. The Jesus Exchange ministry welcomes Christ's own life into ours—His holiness in place of our sin, His blessing in exchange for our curse, His freedom for our captivity. I'm nourished and thrilled by every thought and experience of this divine exchange that Bill heralds so well.

While *The Jesus Exchange* isn't a theological treatise, Dr. Day ably challenges the traditional, Western emphasis on Jesus' death more than His life. Though I'm a traditionalist regarding substitutionary atonement, Bill's writing stretches me, and inspires me to think expansively and to embrace the life-giving, saving work of Christ for all it means."

—**Alan D. Wright, senior pastor of Reynolda Church (a multi site congregation in NC), daily radio teacher heard on 400 stations nation-wide, and best-selling author of six books, including most recently *The Power to Bless* and *Seeing as Jesus Sees*.**

"In *The Jesus Exchange*, Dr. Bill Day, a clinical psychologist, brings not only a unique perspective of his own transformation, but also has integrated his discoveries into his ministry and his theological reflections. He invites you to "dive into Jesus." Are you longing to know and feel God's love in a personal way? If so, then I invite you to read *The Jesus Exchange*. You will not be disappointed."

–**Paul Leitzell, executive pastor, Oasis Church, Holly Springs, NC.**

THE JESUS EXCHANGE

An invitation into Real Life

In Him God replaces

∞ lies with truth
∞ broken hearts with healing
∞ self-grasping with self-giving
∞ addiction with freedom
∞ anxiety with peace
∞ disconnection with reconciliation
∞ death with Eternal Life

William J. Day

Copyright © 2024 by William J. Day

Pyramid Publishers
Minneapolis, Minnesota

All rights reserved, including the right to reproduce this book or portions thereof in any form whatsoever, without prior written permission of the author.

ISBN—978-1-7351068-9-2
Cover Painting "Two Hearts Beat As One" Copyright © by Stephen Anderson
   Prints available at: stephen-anderson.pixels.com
Cover Design by Stan Elder
Interior Design and Layout by Pyramid Publishers
Printed in the United States of America

Unless otherwise noted, Scripture quotations are from the Holy Bible, **New King James Version**. Copyright 1979, 1980, 1982 by Thomas Nelson, Inc. Used by permission. All rights reserved.

Scripture quotations noted AMP are from the **Amplified Bible**. Copyright 1954, 1958, 1962, 1964, 1965, 1987 by The Lockman Foundation. Used by permission. All rights reserved.

Scripture quotations noted ESV are from the Holy Bible, **English Standard Version**. Copyright 2001 by Crossway, a publishing ministry of Good news Publishers. Used by permission. All rights reserved.

Scripture quotations noted NASB are from the **New American Standard Bible**. Copyright 1960, 1962, 1963, 1968, 1971, 1972, 1973, 1975, 1977, 1994 by The Lockman Foundation. Used by permission. All rights reserved.

Scripture quotations noted NIV are from the Holy Bible, **New International Version**. Copyright 1973, 1978, 1984 by Zondervan Publishing House. Used by permission. All rights reserved.

Scripture quotations noted LEB are from the **Lexham English Bible**. Copyright 2010, 2012, 2013 by Lexham Press. Used by permission. All rights reserved.

INTRODUCTION

The Gospel is an invitation into a relationship.

While writing my first two books, *Healing Troubled Hearts* (2014) and *Becoming the Likeness of Jesus* (2018), a vivid scene repeatedly opened before my mind's eye. The scene was a semi-darkened church interior, and a few men and women were sitting in its pews. It was a somber scene, the figures sitting stiffly, looking rather mirthless. Each person was holding a piece of paper in their fingers, gripping the paper tightly, half of it protruding from the top of their fingers. As I looked more closely, I realized that they were holding tickets. Suddenly the meaning of the scene unfolded; it was as though the picture came out of pause-mode and into motion as a narrative of what was going on inside their souls.

The people in the pews had accepted Jesus Christ as their Savior, but He wasn't really part of daily life. Their lives were mostly filled with attempts to achieve standards of morality and principled living, most often ending with them feeling that they had come up short, that they had not measured up. Continuous cycles of trying and failing had left them frustrated and anxious. They believed that this earthly life is all about gritting one's teeth and bearing up under it until their dying day. After death they could hand over their tickets in exchange for the peace and joy awaiting them in heaven.

So, they held tightly to their tickets, clinging to a belief in what Jesus made possible for them by dying for their sins. Yes, they were forgiven, but they were living without a sense that in His Incarnation, Jesus had ventured deep into the interior of fallen human nature so that He could change it from the inside. In this broader picture of the Incarnation, Jesus is viewed as having accomplished something *within Himself*, and *within us* now as we abide in Him.

While writing both previous books, each time this scene appeared in my mind, part of its unfolding was the Holy Spirit whispering about the transformative nature of the Gospel, way beyond garnering a ticket to heaven. What I hope to give expression to in this volume is that, far more substantive than exchanging a ticket for a place within the Pearly Gates, the divine exchange of *2 Corinthians 5:21* is also aptly called the great exchange because it is so extensive in its scope and effect.

I have come to the point of believing that the exchange articulated in *2 Corinthians 5:21* is the heart of the Gospel: "For He made Him who knew no sin to be sin for us, that we might become the righteousness of God in Him." Part of this discovery is that The Gospel is an invitation into a relationship with Jesus Christ, and that within this relationship He imparts His righteous human nature into us, and we gradually become like Him. Through this relationship with Jesus, we are thereby invited into the relational life of our three-persons God (*2 Peter* 1:4).

"Gospel" means a good message, good news. Jesus Christ is the living Word (News) of God. He speaks to the inhabitants of the entire earth the most powerful good news we could ever hear, that we were created by a God who is *holy love*. As such, the core disposition of God's heart is always inclined lovingly towards us and for us, never against us, even if *holy love* means eradication of anything that is unholy.

The Jesus Exchange is an evidence-based investigation into the assertion that the Gospel is an invitation to take up residence within Jesus, as a branch within the Vine of true life (*John* 15:5). My research and discovery have mostly taken place over the past 14 years, weaving together three threads of exploration: (1) Scriptures of Old and New Testaments, (2) the manifest laws of God in nature and written on our hearts, and (3) testimonies of scores of patients, including myself as a patient.

In citing Scripture as the primary thread of exploration, I have especially endeavored to adhere to two of the most orienting verses in the Bible: *Hebrews* 12:2, ". . . fixing our eyes on Jesus," because He is "the express image of God's nature" (*Hebrews* 1:3).

A second thread of exploration is that the laws of science and nature are derived from and expressive of the overarching design feature in all creation: The Law of Love. This thread will manifest its golden hue throughout the book.

The third thread of exploration is that of experience. As a Christian psychologist and pastoral counselor, my experiential context is the spiritual warfare and healing that have taken place in my life and in the lives of my patients in the past 30 years. Counseling settings have included church-based ministry and outpatient psychotherapy practices.

The views expressed in *The Jesus Exchange* are not intended to be arguments against other views. They are my discoveries in a continuous search for truth. Seeking truth has been a significant driving force in my own life; this book is a way of sharing what I have discovered so far.

If you are exploring the journey of wanting to know more about what an immersion of one's life into Christ Jesus means or whether such an immersion is even possible, I hope you will find this book both enlightening and enlivening.

ACKNOWLEDGMENT

I have tried to make the writing readily readable rather than awkwardly academic. To whatever extent it flows and hangs together coherently I credit my cadre of readers and editors, especially the final editor, my wife, Susan. She is currently a professional pet sitter but has taken a side job as one of my editors. She no doubt finds it easier to work with her dogs, cats, and bunnies than laboring as an editor with me, so I want to thank her publicly for generously partnering with me, as she does in so many ways in our life together. Thanks, My Love, for sure it's a better book because of you.

TABLE OF CONTENTS

INTRODUCTION   The Gospel is an invitation into a relationship.

ACKNOWLEDGMENT

TABLE OF CONTENTS

BEFORE YOU BEGIN

PART I: A STORY OF SEARCHING FOR HEALING AND TRUTH
Chapter 1 Real Healing..1
Chapter 2 Long Day's Journey into Night..8
Chapter 3 Dawn Breaks Through..17
Chapter 4 A New Day..22
Chapter 5 Exchanges For Life: Jesus Exchange Ministry........................31

PART II: DISCOVERING THE LARGER STORY
Chapter 6 God's Plan: Out with the Old, In with the New.....................47
Chapter 7 Fixing Our Eyes Fully on Jesus..56
Chapter 8 Rescuing Us From the Miry Pit...60
Chapter 9 Reclaiming What Had Been Stolen...65
Chapter 10 The Divine Dilemma...73
Chapter 11 The Death of Sin and the Sin-prone Old Self.......................82
Chapter 12 A Whole Lot of Pouring Going On.......................................90
Chapter 13 A Tale of Two Facets..94
Chapter 14 Arise, My Son!..102

DISCOVERY GEMS..115

RESOURCES..123

AFTERWORD..127

APPENDIX I   Interacting with God, Observations and Guidelines....129

BIBLIOGRAPHY...135

BEFORE YOU BEGIN

- I have been given permission to disclose the contents of the therapy sessions I use, but names and some personal details of patients have been changed.

- Although I directly quote from the Bible and cite the sources of verses in the text of any given chapter, I do not reference or quote authors from whom I have adapted ideas. I do this to smooth the flow of the narrative for easier reading. I acknowledge my sources for each chapter in a later section of the book titled RESOURCES.

- Disclosure statement: Although I share interventions and strategies for dealing with emotional and spiritual issues, this book is not a formal treatment manual. Readers are cautioned about the potential risk of using limited knowledge when integrating new methods into practice.

PART I

A STORY OF SEARCHING FOR HEALING AND TRUTH

A thread that weaves throughout this book is the dynamic within the imagery of an exchange transfusion. From birth, I was filled with the religion of Christianity, as the doctrines and teachings of Roman Catholicism (original "donor blood") were poured into my mind. In my 20s, I added to this deposit by pouring in tenets of liberal Protestantism. In my late 20s, I flushed out the entire deposit of the religion of Christianity, replacing it with atheistic Secular Humanism. I lived within the principles and beliefs of Secular Humanism until this deposit came crashing to a dead end and became waste material within my soul. As Secular Humanism drained out of my life, I discovered new "donor blood" that poured in as I drank deeply of the supposed heavenly elixir of New Age Spirituality. For 14 years I lived in this world, until I was invited to participate in flushing out New Age Spirituality and my entire old life, in exchange for a new life in Christ Jesus.

I chose to accept this invitation, a choice that has turned out to be the turning point in my life. At 42 years of age, healing began as I allowed the Holy Spirit to begin flushing old life from my body, soul, and spirit. New life poured in, and continues to pour in as this exchange transfusion has become the core dynamic of my daily life.

The first five chapters are a summary of these many exchanges, setting the stage for the discoveries of the larger story of the Incarnation in PART II.

Chapter 1

Real Healing

The woman walked slowly into my office and slumped down into a chair as if she were carrying the weight of the world on her shoulders. She looked as though she hadn't slept well for several weeks or months, her eyes red-rimmed with exhaustion.

Nancy was a pleasant-looking woman in her mid-forties, but her complexion was pale and her makeup couldn't hide the lines of worry etched into her face or the dark shadows of weariness drooping under her eyes.

"Dr. Day," she began in a voice barely above a whisper, "I need your help." Her voice spoke out desperation, but hope flickered in her eyes communicating a belief that just maybe I could help her.

Her husband, Tom, had come in with her and took a chair slightly off to the side. He had a quiet demeanor, looking at his wife as though he was her bodyguard, ready to protect her from harm. The focus was clearly on her.

Nancy began her story by recounting an event that had happened eight months previously, while driving to meet a client. She was an interior decorator, working in the Raleigh, North Carolina area for the past several years. Suddenly, without warning, she felt grabbed by a panic attack: intense fear, pounding heart, shaking, shortness of breath, and sweating. Dizziness and fear seized her and she felt she was about to go crazy, or even die. She pulled off the road shortly after the attack began, and when it passed, she caught her breath and returned to work, though badly shaken by the event.

Nancy shifted nervously in her chair as she proceeded to tell me that several more panic attacks occurred over the next six weeks. She would be afraid of having an attack, and that would bring on another attack. She also had intermittent anxiety unrelated to anything except the anticipation of having another panic attack.

She was worn out from the struggle and was just waiting for the next time the claws of fear would spring out and grab her again.

During the weeks after the first attack, Nancy had sought help from a psychiatrist and a psychotherapist and was currently taking two medications. The medications had slowed down the frequency of the attacks, but the undercurrent of anxiety was always there. The psychotherapy did not seem to be helping.

Nancy said she did not know if her problem had any spiritual basis, but she was a Christian and wanted a Christian counselor. She added that she was desperate and knew she needed God's power to get through what had become the crisis of her life.

She had quit her job and had become a recluse, sitting at home with the curtains closed. She could not drive anymore. Her husband, an avid fisherman, enjoyed going to the coast on fishing trips. However, she could not tolerate him being more than 50 miles away without having a wave of anxiety. She felt sad that he couldn't go fishing any more. Her husband spoke up to say that he was willingly sacrificing his hobby, he just wanted her to get well. Though they did not say so, it was clear that this crisis was a strain on their marriage. There was heaviness in the air.

Both Nancy and Tom were carrying heavy burdens and had showed up at my doorstep for help. An alleviation of symptoms would not do here, and I began to feel a burden myself.

"Nothing is too big for God," I said. I could hear the uncertainty in my voice and wondered if they could hear it as well. Evidently those were the words she wanted to hear. She smiled weakly and said she would like to begin therapy. An appointment was set for the following week.

On the day of her appointment, Nancy returned looking about the same as she had the week before. I turned from my desk and rolled my chair around to face her. Her husband once again sat off to the side, watching.

Nancy began describing a chaotic childhood with an early breakup between her mother and father. After Nancy's father exited, she lived with her mother, whom she described as having a serious alcohol problem coupled with significant mental health issues. She recounted an early memory at age four, in which she was standing outside the front door of a house, suitcase by her side, watching her mother walk away and then drive off. Her mother was evidently unable to cope with her problems and raise Nancy, so she gave her away to her childless sister and brother-in-law who lived in another town.

Nancy then described the ranch-style house of her aunt and uncle. Their bedroom was at one end of the house and Nancy's at the other end. She said they were stern folks. As an example, she told of having to sleep at night in her bedroom without having any light on, even from the nearby bathroom. She had been afraid of the dark as long as she could remember. Despite Nancy's repeated pleas, her aunt and uncle would not relent.

She said, "I have memories of lying in my bed, covers pulled up to my chin, just scared to death." At this point in the session, she closed her eyes without any direction from me, perhaps because the memory was so strong and vivid.

I asked, "Were you alone there?" "Yes," she said. "My aunt and uncle were either in the living room or had gone to bed. I didn't know which because they always closed my door."

What happened next will sound odd to your ears, as it did to mine. "Was anyone else there?" I asked. I immediately felt foolish. Nancy had just told me she was alone. Why had I asked such a dumb question?

"No one, I was alone."

My self-talk was, *move on with her story, she said she was alone and feeling very afraid.*

I was about to push on into having her describe more of her life in that home, when, still with eyes closed, she said, "Oh . . . God was there!" Her face brightened as she was seeing something happen in the memory. "The whole room is filled with light, and Jesus is standing next to my bed. I know it is Him." Moments passed. "He is touching my arm and telling me that He loves me and that He'll always be with me and take care of me."

A long pause. "All the fear is gone," she finally said. "All the fear is gone, and I just feel so peaceful."

I was startled and looked over at Tom. He too was absorbing what was taking place. No longer watching from the sideline, he looked to be drawn into what was occurring, though he was clearly startled.

I did not know what to do next. Nancy opened her eyes and began to weep copious tears of relief and joy. It was as though she had been released from a dark dungeon. She was overcome with relief after long years of living in the grip of fear. Her tears were those of release and freedom.

Coming out of my own absorption in this scene, my mind slowly cleared. I focused, and then like the sharp peal of a bell going off in my brain, I astutely knew what to do next . . . I handed Nancy a box of Kleenex. That was easily the most significant contribution I made to the proceedings that day.

The session drew to a close and another appointment was set for the following week. Nancy and Tom had much to assimilate, as did I. Somehow I knew that things would never be the same for all three of us.

When Nancy and Tom returned the following week, I began by asking her how she was doing. Although a habituated heaviness was still present in much of her body language, there was light in her eyes and new energy in her voice.

She first said that the memory of being alone at night in the darkened bedroom had changed. She still had a sense of Jesus' presence there and the room was filled with light. Several times she had tried in her mind to make the bedroom dark again, but she could not. And she added that the fear was completely gone. Words of amazement were exchanged and then Nancy continued with her life story.

The rest of the story

As you might imagine, Nancy had lots of anxiety and fear packed into her early years. Rejection and abandonment created a sense of isolation, and she always felt on the outside looking in. Her sense of self-confidence and self-worth was very low, and she found her way into peer groups in which the members also saw themselves as outsiders. She had not gone off the deep end into drugs and promiscuity, but in her younger years she found alcohol and food to be useful pain relievers and comforters.

Early on in their marriage, she and her husband had joined a church. Both became involved in church activities and services, but she always felt an emotional distance from God. She tried to please Him by behaving well, though when she failed, she always felt anxious and guilty because she believed she had disappointed Him.

During the next six weeks of therapy, unusual and unprecedented healing occurred. Nancy did not again have a visual manifestation of Jesus in her memories, but she felt a sense of His presence seep into her memories as she continued telling her story. It was as though He was there, walking with her through her whole life—from the initial sense of standing next to her in the bedroom memory to walking with her in the subsequent events of her life.

For example, she would be describing a scene in adolescence, talking about how lonely and dejected she felt . . . and then she would interject, "Oh, but Jesus was there." She would pause for a few moments, close her eyes, and let that realization enter the memory. The feelings in the memory would change from negative to positive feelings of peace. Sometimes she would report hearing quiet words of love and comfort.

Nancy simply let the presence of the Lord come into each event in her life as she recounted it. He dissolved the anxiety, boosted her fragile self-image, and removed doubts about her prospects for the future. I was witnessing someone come alive before my eyes, as we talked through her life, year by year, right up to the present moment.

In her memories, she experienced being loved and valued rather than being rejected. It was a swap-out, an exchanged-life process that was actual, not merely conceptual. There was no therapeutic task of getting truth or positive thoughts from her head to her heart. As I saw it, she had opened her simple faith to acknowledge the truth that God was in that bedroom with her, as well as in all the events of her life. He walked right in through the open portal of her faith, and from there He entered any soul room (memory) in which she came to the door and said, "Come in."

As the weeks went by, I often thought of the passage in *Revelation* 3:20 NIV: "Here I am! I stand at the door and knock. If anyone hears my voice and opens the door, I will come in and eat with that person, and they with me." Nancy heard Jesus' voice, kept opening doors for Him to come in, and eagerly savored the delicious meal of His presence.

Within three months, and after 10 therapy sessions, Nancy had discontinued all her medications without any severe withdrawal symptoms.[1] She had no more panic attacks. She returned to her work, driving there herself. The last time she came to my office, she came without her husband and looked like a different person. The weary look, the forlorn voice, and the shuffling gait were gone. She was full of life and energy, and light beamed from her eyes.

At the end of the session, she agreed to call me on an as-needed basis. As she was walking through the doorway of the office, she turned around and said, "Tom has gone back to his fishing at the coast." She smiled, turned, and left. I smiled at the thought of Tom out there fishing, enjoying his freedom in the surf and the wind.

I never saw Nancy or Tom again, but I did receive a phone call from Nancy several years later. Though they had moved out of state, she had been in touch with a friend in North Carolina who was experiencing emotional difficulties. Nancy said that she wanted to refer her friend to see me and wondered if I was taking new patients. "But, before we talk about that, I want to tell you something." She paused, and then emphatically said, "I'm still healed!"

She updated me on her life: She never had another panic attack, and her life kept getting better in many ways. She then said again, "I'm healed."

Nancy concluded her update by sharing that she was now in ministry as a speaker for women's conferences and retreats within her denomination. When asked what she spoke on, she said, "I just tell my story of how love cast out fear."

In the moment she said that last sentence, a shaft of light pen-

---

[1] Nancy was weaned off her medications under the guidance of her psychiatrist. This is always the safe way to proceed. I believe that sometimes there can be severe physiological imbalances in brain chemistry that require extended use of medication. This was not the case with Nancy.

etrated my mind with the wondrous ways of God. He knew Nancy would be burdened for years with anxiety that seemingly wasted her time and energy. However, He patiently awaited the days when she would turn her heart and her whole life over to Him, knowing that He would transform and enliven her, and enrich the lives of others through her.

The *First Epistle of John* 4:18 says, ". . . perfect love casts out fear." That portion of Scripture was no longer just words on a page, it was living in Nancy. She was a witness to that truth, and her life now had a purpose beyond herself—to share this truth with others. She ended her phone call by saying how fulfilling it was to be launched into the purposes God had intended for her all along.

This true story of Nancy happened in 1995. It was my first in-depth experience of real transformation in a patient's life, though I had been working in the field of mental health for many years. In my time with Nancy, I had witnessed a great exchange of love replacing fear, truth replacing lies, and a sense of purpose replacing a chaotic struggle to survive brokenness.

It was the beginning of a discovery process that is the subject of this book. Things were never the same for me after Nancy. At the time of Nancy's healing, I was just emerging from many years of being lost. Like Nancy, I was riddled with anxiety, struggling to survive.

Within me was hidden a similar story of fear needing to be cast out of the soul and replaced with love.

Chapter 2

Long Day's Journey into Night

Before I came along, to avoid having another child, my Roman Catholic parents were practicing the rhythm method of birth control (abstaining from sex during ovulation). Times were tight economically and my father thought that two children, a boy and a girl, were enough. At the same time, my mother was secretly praying for the favor of a child. Within this ambivalence I was conceived and was born on February 4, 1942. A younger brother arrived 18 months later.

Soon after my birth, my maternal grandmother came for a visit and informed my parents that she had a dream in which it was shown to her that I had a "special destiny" in life. My parents and extended family interpreted her dream as a sure sign of the most special destiny for an Irish Catholic son: to be a priest.

Life in a bubble

Growing up I did not have a thought of becoming anything other than a priest, and I accepted that this was my destiny. On one hand I had a sense of belonging to an elite group, a sense of having a highly valued vocation waiting for me in the future. On the other hand, I had few experiences of just being a flesh-and-blood boy, belonging to a human family. All my family members, teachers, and friends knew that I would be leaving for the seminary after finishing elementary school.

Kind though my parents were, there was a reserve in them towards me. I experienced them more as guardians, taking care of me until it would be time for me to leave home after eighth grade. I felt different from everyone else; all my friends, and even my siblings seemed somewhat at arms' length. Being special had definite advantages—like receiving a deluxe tricycle with a big fur seat from a family friend who was a bishop in Kentucky—but there was also isolation.

I did not consciously experience the isolation, but there were recurring nightmares. I would wake up screaming in fear. My father would come into my bedroom and take me out into the hallway. Pulling up a chair, he held me in his lap until I calmed down and could return to bed. I could not really describe to my father why I was so frightened. The nightmares were different each time, but the feeling I had was the same terrifying fear.

In retrospect, it seems clear that the emotion in each recurrent nightmare was separation anxiety generated from a lack of basic human attachment. This buried anxiety would burst through the lowered veil of consciousness during sleep, manifesting itself in fear-laced nightmares. My father physically holding me in the hallway calmed my anxiety, momentarily resolving my sense of detachment. The anxiety would abate, like stirred-up sediment in a river settling back onto a riverbed. In the morning, life would return to "normal."

While in therapy in my thirties, a psychotherapist guided me to walk consciously into one of those remembered nightmares, and then I "got it." In the dreams, I was in a transparent bubble. I could see people, animals, etc., through the bubble, but couldn't hear, smell, or touch anything. I was alone in the bubble, and the feeling that would wake me was fear. No connection, no attachment, no sense of belonging. It was dark and scary in there.

The seminary

My time to leave home came after finishing elementary school in 1956. I was 14 years old. My father drove me from Detroit Lakes, Minnesota to Holy Cross Seminary in La Crosse, Wisconsin, a journey of 350 miles.

The adventure had begun, and, after the initial shock, I felt a gradual sense of belonging. This was my band of brothers with whom I could join in the high-call adventure of becoming a priest. However, the arrow of disconnection stayed firmly in place, in that we seminarians were given strict admonition against forming "particular friendships." Scripture was used to reinforce the warning. We were told that *1 Corinthians* 9:22 pertained to us: to ". . . become all things to all men." As priests we would need to be servants to all members of the flock, and therefore not be attached to any person in particular. I followed the guidelines and developed a detached relationship style.

I fully accepted my identity as a priest-to-be. This was my life. This was me. I returned home to Minnesota for vacations, but with each passing vacation, I looked more and more forward to the end of vacation, when I could return to my "real home" in the seminary. However, upon returning to the seminary in the fall of my junior year in college, I was shocked when serious doubts about my vocation suddenly surfaced. It wasn't about missing girls or missing anything on the outside; it was more like someone had taken away a precious, shining jewel from inside of me when I wasn't looking.

I didn't know why the jewel had been removed, but I no longer felt like I was destined to be a priest, and I couldn't figure out what had happened. I consulted my spiritual director and other priests, all of whom tried to dispel my doubts—to no avail.

I had not been taught how to talk to or listen to God in an informal, non-structured way, so He seemed silent and remote to me. I finished my senior year of college at Holy Cross, but all sense of belonging had disappeared. The jewel was gone, the adventure was over, and I was no longer a member of the band of brothers.

I was a stranger in a strange land and there was no adventure waiting for me. In my perception, there was nothing waiting for me. I had to leave the seminary, and I felt a sense of shame. I had been a relatively good seminarian, but evidently something was missing. A powerful *arrow of rejection* pierced my heart. It went in quickly and silently, under the radar of consciousness . . . and it went deep.

The year was 1964. I walked out of the seminary and into the world, free from the external confines of the seminary. However, I was wounded and bound up on the inside with pain, fear, and anger, a fact I didn't acknowledge for a long while. The seminary had been a way of life, not just a school. Gone was any sense of belonging. In a flash, my identity vanished. I was a young man stripped of a sense of purpose, and as soon as I walked outside the walls of that seminary into the world, a cavernous sinkhole opened inside of me.

I had developed into a thoroughly self-centered person, a state that would stubbornly stay in place for the next 20 years. However well-intentioned the nuns and priests might have been in my elementary, high school, and college education, I walked out of Holy Cross Seminary as an insulated, isolated, narrow-minded man. And, characteristic of pride, I was so bound up in myself that I couldn't see my true condition.

Journeys in and out of darkness

The next 20 years can be characterized as multiple attempts to break out of "the bubble." These phases were intermittent spurts of energy as I staggered from one upheaval to another, from one worldview into another, from one career dead-end into a hopeful new direction . . . only to result in yet another complete swap-out because the new light dimmed into darkness.

1. The death of Christian religion. After leaving the seminary, I entered Marquette University in Milwaukee, Wisconsin and earned a master's degree in theology. My intention was to become a lay theologian, a kind of "whistling in the dark" attempt to fill the awful void created by the loss of my priest-identity.

In the seminary, and continuing at Marquette, there was endless God-talk in classes, retreats, and sermons. There seemed to be a mysterious kind of assumption in play—that somehow, we were making God present by *talking* about Him. I don't know if I thought that ideas about God would somehow make their way down into my heart and out into my life by osmosis. But *knowing about* a loving God did not translate into a loving relationship with God or with others.

After receiving my master's degree at Marquette, I taught theology for two years at university level. Taking leading thoughts from the liberal theology taught at Marquette, I began to explore the many challenges to Christian orthodoxy that were developing in the years after the seemingly progressive Second Vatican Council ended in 1964.

However, I hadn't developed a personal relationship with Jesus, and before the end of my second year of teaching, I had discarded Catholicism—indeed, the entire worldview of Christianity was dissipating within my soul. I had swapped out Catholicism for a liberal Protestant perspective, and from there had embraced death-of-institutional-Christianity theology—essentially working my way out of a career as a Christian theologian! I began to feel a dreadful emptiness inside once again. However, nature abhors a vacuum, and a powerful replacement soon arrived.

2. The rise and fall of the secular self. Without much forethought, I resigned my teaching position and enrolled in a master's degree program in social work at San Diego State University in Southern California. By the end of my first year there, the soul void was filled by an immersion into the theories of psychologists Carl Rogers, Abraham Maslow, Albert Ellis, and many others who had developed the theme of *self-actualization*. For someone who inwardly felt that his *self* had been hijacked since birth, these initially seemed to be refreshing waters to swim in.

I filled my vacated mind with these "liberating" ideas. Self-realization and self-actualization replaced the need for salvation. Christianity had been poured into me; I had taken it in but never really wrestled with it or willingly chose it. It was not difficult, at least consciously, to let all the doctrines drain out and be replaced with a psychology that seemed to be healing and life-giving.

By the end of my two years in San Diego, I had replaced the religion of Christianity with the religion of Humanism (though at the time I did not think of it as a religion). Through experimenting with drugs like marijuana and mescaline, my perceptions were supposedly lining up with "reality." To complete this version of out-with-the-old and in-with-the-new, my first marriage ended after less than two years and no children. Promiscuity filled that empty space, and I thought of the new relationships simply as more positive steps towards self-actualization.

There were some unpleasant changes. When relationships would end (and especially if rejection was involved), it would tap into the reservoir of pain hidden in my heart, and powerful emotions of anger, sadness, and fear would well up. Anxiety from a lifelong lack of human attachment and pain from my seminary rejection wound poured out—like ripples from stones that had been thrown into the pond of my life years ago.

In the safety of a humanistic psychologist's office, I began to uncover the seething turmoil underneath the surface. But the therapists I saw only provided *insight* into the deeper issues but not *healing*. So, I would get patched up and then move along to the next adventure. In 1970, after graduating from San Diego State University, the next adventure was Napa, California.

Napa hit me smack in the face with a part of life I had not seen. Along with a classmate from San Diego, I was hired by Napa County to open a Child Protection Services unit. My tidy world of self-realization and opening my "doors of perception" through drug use was soberly shaken by the reality of an alcoholic father putting out lit cigarettes on his three-year-old son's back, by parents punching and kicking their children into submission, and by the horrors of child sexual abuse.

Day after day I witnessed this dark side of life, and the tools in my clinical toolbox were woefully inadequate to deal with any of it. I used what I was taught, applying soul bandages here and there, and "managing" situations to prevent further damage from occurring. But after a year, I was totally discouraged.

Tremendous confusion grew inside of me. In my San Diego classrooms, I had been taught that self-actualization could be achieved without much conflict, and that the intrinsic goodness of the human self would come through once people saw the truth of innate human goodness. However, in real-life Napa, I encountered extensive self-hatred, despair, and hopelessness in my Napa clients, not people on a journey to self-actualization.

Intuitively I knew that the evil I encountered was not coming solely from external forces such as authoritarian government, a restrictive moral code, or bad parenting. This dark stuff was seeping out from deep inside the souls of the many people I encountered. Within just a few months, my humanistic/hippie understanding of life was on very shaky ground.

Another reality caught me by surprise. My own unresolved pain, anger, and anxiety were triggered and brought to the surface by exposure to daily doses of unresolved relational turmoil in the lives of my clients. The net effect of this triggering was a gradual amplification of *my* inner turmoil, heading towards a breaking point.

During that year in Napa, I increasingly felt as though I was inside a room in which all four walls were slowly but inexorably closing in on me. It felt as though my first 20 years of life were the bricks in the walls, and none of the exchanges and decisions I had made in subsequent years had dealt with these "bricks." I was in my 29th year and the walls were closing in on me.

Having no anchor and no sense of direction left me feeling fearfully lost. I decided to leave everything and travel abroad. Embarking on a journey wasn't just about getting away for a while. It seemed that the entirety of my old life was failing and collapsing. I wanted to shed this old life and exchange it for a new one. In the hippie jargon of the day, I was setting out to *find myself*.

3. A deeper darkness. Although much of my wandering abroad was aimless, as a late-blooming hippie I moved within communities of like-minded people, of which there were many in the early 1970s. Part of "getting lost" was stripping away any connection to religion, but while traveling I began to take an interest in a new worldview that permeated much of the hippie culture.

According to many popular proponents of astrology, Earth entered the Age of Aquarius sometime in the 19th century. Since an astrological age is about 2,160 years long, by 1971 Earth was supposedly just getting started in this New Age. The astrological sign of Aquarius is a man pouring spiritual water out of a large vessel. The in-vogue interpretation of this sign was that the hallmark of the Age of Aquarius would be an outpouring of truth and an expansion of consciousness. This would be the age in which humankind would take control of its own destiny, evolving into its rightful divine heritage.

The basic beliefs of this New Age worldview can be summarized as follows: We are all divine. We are God, we just don't know it yet. What we call God is everywhere, in everyone and everything. We search all over the world (as I was doing) and right here, already inside us is this "dozing Divinity," waiting to be discovered and awakened.

New Age spirituality planted itself into my wandering soul and took root. For a while I felt on track to truth and freedom. I stopped doing drugs and strove to overcome my ego and ascend into the divine realm, the "Higher Self."

While in India I spent time in the ashram of an Indian guru. I learned and practiced several meditation techniques, trying to see down into my "Divinity" with my spiritual "third eye." Back in Europe I also studied and practiced other forms of spirituality. I absorbed and practiced New Age beliefs, but they did not bring peace. The pre-travel panic feelings were gone, and that was a relief, but I still felt deeply unsettled.

4. More lost than ever. After returning to the United States, I spent the next 10 years striving to find peace for my anxious soul. I made a second trip abroad to study and live in a "Spiritual Science" community. For three years I lived in this community, entering into a second marriage and fathering a son through this union.

Shortly after returning from this second trip abroad, I enrolled in a doctoral program in clinical psychology, at the Center for Humanistic Studies, in Detroit, Michigan, where I discovered that many of my former mentors in humanistic psychology had embraced New Age spirituality and declared that *real* self-actualization involved merging with the *Higher Self*. Shedding their humanistic views, they had become enlightened "transpersonal psychologists." I read their new books, picked up the new drumbeat, and began following in their footsteps.

By 1984, after all my study, striving, practicing meditation, and pursuing spiritually based healing methods, no real transformation had taken place. During my second trip abroad, a therapist guided me into a better understanding of the childhood nightmares I described in Chapter 1. But understanding what was going on in the nightmares neither removed the fear nor removed me from "the bubble." I could not will myself out of it. I was still locked up inside myself, in a bubble of isolation.

Relationally, my life was a disaster. I had gone from one relationship to another, from one marriage to another, subconsciously trying to heal the deep detachment wound from my childhood. I kept trying to attach, to belong, to be close to someone. Bumbling in and out of relationships, I was now headed towards a third marriage.

In short, my life was a mess. My journeys to *find myself* were journeys to nowhere. I did not acknowledge it as such, but I was treading water, hanging on, hoping that my involvements in a new relationship and a new doctoral program in psychology would get me up and swimming. Life had become more complicated than ever before, with children now added to the mix.

Weariness was slowly settling into body and soul as I continued treading water. I returned to occasional marijuana use to numb the pain and tone down the constant undercurrent of anxiety. I was indeed more lost than ever, yet in almost total denial about the true state of my soul.

Chapter 3

Dawn Breaks Through

In late autumn of 1984, in a suburb of Detroit, Michigan, I had accepted an invitation to attend a church service, more out of curiosity than anything else.

I remember well that Wednesday evening service at Brightmoor Tabernacle, an Assemblies of God church. I had never been in a Protestant church before, so at first I felt strange sitting there in the pew, faintly feeling the reprimand my parents would have given for attending a Protestant church. However, those feelings were quickly dispelled as the pastor launched into the Last Supper discourse from the *Gospel of John*.

I had heard many sermons in my life but nothing like this one. The pastor skillfully opened up passage after passage, letting the theme of God's love for us exude from the verses like a delicate fragrance. In those moments I was touched on the inside by something that somehow made its way past my protective walls and defenses.

The sermon was not a transmission of knowledge from the pastor's head to my head. His words were coming from his *heart*, and I felt energized and enlivened in my heart. Driving home that evening, I realized that I had just heard the best sermon of my life.

I returned on Sunday for the full service. Although my curiosity was piqued by Wednesday's sermon, I was still wary of being in a Protestant church. My usual mindset had settled back into a defensive, critical mode, and skeptically I watched about 500 people talking in the aisles and beginning to fill the pews. I felt as though I was on the *inside* of reality, and these church folks were on the outside, in some weird religious world.

The service began. Within ten minutes, in an utterly startling shift, my perception completely flipped: *They* were on the inside of something I intuitively felt was real and alive, and *I* was on the outside.

In that moment, at age 42, I had my first authentic encounter with God.

A clearly authoritative, yet gentle voice said, "I am life." I did not hear the voice audibly with my ears, yet I somehow perceived the words within me, and they were being spoken by a person. I had a sense of a personal presence other than myself. It was not the voice of my self-talk chattering away as it did throughout the day. This voice was clearly distinct from myself yet communicating with me.

As those words were spoken, a remarkable thing happened. Like a fog lifting, I saw that everything I was attached to—the drugs, the hippie lifestyle, my New Age beliefs, my frantic search for knowledge—all comprised something like a pseudo life-support machine into which I was plugged. I could see and feel the tangled tubes attaching me to those things, and I knew that this whole life-support system was pseudo life not real life.

Then a gentle but firm understanding came into my mind: *You can choose what to have as life—Me or the life-supports to which you are attached.* The tone and meaning of the proposal were crystal clear: it was an invitation, and I somehow sensed that this was a God invitation. But it was a one-or-the-other exchange, I could not have it both ways. I had to choose what would be *life* for me. There was a sobering pause as I absorbed this realization. Then, inwardly I said, "I choose You."

At that time, I didn't know what name would describe Whom I had encountered: God, Creator, Ultimate Reality, The Source. C.S. Lewis sometimes referred to God as "The Real," and there in Brightmoor Tabernacle such a name made sense.

I had been shown that I was living in unreality and calling it reality. My entire perception had been flipped and reversed. With different eyes I watched the people singing and praying during the rest of the Sunday service. They were not religious nuts playing church and going through mechanical motions. I could see that they were experiencing something real, and they knew it. They were alive.

I had an impulse to bow down to the Person who spoke to me, who was in this church and involved with these people. I was in the presence of an awesome Being, yet this Being was personal and inviting.

At the time, I did not fully respond to the invitation, but I took the first step by going home and throwing away all my marijuana and drug paraphernalia. That drug had been my major "life-support"; disconnecting from it was a major step.

Below the surface

It didn't happen magically or immediately, but a new dynamic was set into motion. I felt a glimpse of hope. Yes, over the years I had pursued several seemingly bright lights that had dimmed and then darkened. There were so many "identities" begun and ended, so many hopes and dreams that had vaporized, so many dead ends.

Counterfeits that promised healing and wholeness had already deceived me several times in my search for truth. Only the desire to know real truth kept drawing me forward from the dead-ends and failures of my many searches. I began to investigate this new light to see if it was *real* light. I began to engage with this person who claimed to be Life. I wanted to discover whether this life was real.

I strongly sensed that the Person I had encountered in Brightmoor Tabernacle was the Trinitarian God of the Bible, and after a preparatory class I accepted the Gospel of Jesus Christ and was baptized, full-immersion style. It was a decision to exchange my old life for this new life. It didn't feel like a re-entry into the religion of Christianity; I had an uncanny sense of entering a new *relationship*. I felt drawn towards a God who apparently wanted to engage personally. This was new territory for me and seemed worthy of exploration.

Two years later, in 1986, After relocating from Michigan to North Carolina, the numbing of my "life-support system" was steadily wearing off. New Age spirituality lost its deceptive sheen as I absorbed the new reality into which I had been immersed. It was time for a heavy dose of reality.

While attending a church in the town of Chapel Hill, at the direction of some men who were mentoring me, I fasted and prayed for over two weeks, consuming only fluids. Afterwards I met with the men, and they asked me what God had shown me during those weeks. I began to tell them my life-story, and at the end, through my disclosure and their comments, I experienced a staggering conviction of the depth of my self-centeredness.

It was like looking below the surface of a huge iceberg to encompass its true size. What I saw was overwhelmingly massive. I broke down into tears for a long time, confronted soberly by the pervasiveness of my pride, arrogance, and sense of entitlement. I cringed at what I saw of the judgmental, lustful, petty, impatient, utterly selfish state of my soul.

I felt helpless. In that moment, like none before, I knew I needed a Savior. The name Jesus made complete sense to me, beyond what I had experienced in Michigan after my conversion experience. I now knew who Jesus was at a deeper level than before, and I knew how desperately I needed Him.

As a humanistic psychologist, I had thrown out the word *sin* along with my old theology books. As a New Ager, I had cleverly disguised evil as *ignorance* that could be corrected by enlightened *knowledge*. But in that moment with those men, and in many moments following that event, I began to sense the reality of evil in the world, especially up close and personal—in me.

Seeing such corruption just below the surface of my soul, I began to soberly realize how deeply rooted was my self-deification. For decades, I had fought fiercely for my "independence." Initially, I balked at the thought of fully trusting or relying on anyone, even a Person who said, *I am Life*. For many years, self had been my only master. However, as the rationalizations for my pervasive self-focus began to wear off and be exposed, I became more willing to look at my self-life and see its true character: resentful, critical, fussy, greedy, haughty, touchy, vain—blind to everything except its own gratification.

At this point I did not grasp or accept the necessity of this old self to die. *Crucified* is a "*hard*" word," as the Irish say. My self had been pumped up and had been running the show for many years; it was not inclined to submit to purposes beyond itself. Further, I had no sense of how to shift out of this self-focus, supposing it to be something that I had to do. It wasn't at all clear how my character and personality could change.

At the direction of my mentors at the aforementioned church, I began a process that would take months to complete: flushing out and throwing away my New Age books, paintings, and other New Age paraphernalia, as well as what remained of my humanistic psychology library. It was as though a kind of transfusion was taking place, one in which mindsets and practices were being identified as "waste blood," to be drained out of my soul.

Dawn breaking through: God's choice or my choice?

In Brightmoor Tabernacle, when I said, "I choose You," it was my choice; but in my guarded, selfish little self, I don't think I was capable of so grand and life-changing a decision on my own.

God's sovereignty and the gift of human choice are still mysterious to me, as to how they interweave in human lives. Something happened that day in Brightmoor Tabernacle, and it was clearly God's favor setting the scene, plus my response of yes to God's invitation.

Both favor and human choice were factors, and a deed was done that day which would change my life forever. The prophecy of Zachariah, recorded in the *Gospel of Luke* 1:78-79, was activated in the soul of a man named William Joseph Day when he was 42 years old:

> . . . Through the tender mercy of our God,
> with which the Dayspring from on high has visited us;
> To give light to those who sit in darkness
> and the shadow of death,
> To guide our feet into the way of peace.

Chapter 4

A New Day

While living in North Carolina, I worked in a mental health center and then a smoking cessation clinic. I finished my dissertation and received a PhD in Clinical Psychology in 1987, gradually shifting towards a more spiritual understanding of healing. I began networking in Christian counseling circles, meeting many counselors and pastors in the area, and even began seeing patients privately in a home-office. I read books on Christian counseling, listened to audio tapes, and attended seminars. Finally, I landed a job in a Christian counseling clinic.

What I encountered in the field of Christian counseling was basically the same cognitive therapy of my secular training in psychotherapy. Secular therapy focused on positive thoughts of succeeding and how to manage behavior. Christian counseling simply added into the cognitive mix thoughts from the Bible that focused on God's goodness, provision, and love.

The Scriptures were rich and deep, such as "Be transformed by the renewing of your mind" (*Romans* 12:2), and ". . . it is no longer I who live but Christ lives in me" (*Galatians* 2:20), suggesting significant and thorough change. However, for the most part the therapeutic approach of Christian counseling focused almost solely on *immediate consciousness*, the top layer of the mind. The hidden issues in the heart were seldom addressed.

From God's Word and my own experience, it seemed clear to me that all humans have darkened depths and hidden anxieties in their souls which need to be searched out and exposed by God (*Psalms* 139:23). Yet, most of what I learned and tried to apply from Christian counseling methods were concepts and coping strategies—all in the form of downloading Bible verses and advice from the counselor's mind into the mind of the client.

Being a rookie Christian counselor, I went with the flow of traditional methods. Even though Jesus said, "I am the truth" (*John* 14:6), in the initial methods I learned and practiced, the operative principle was truth = *true cognitive information.*

The rationale seemed to be that if clients, indeed if all Christians, could *push* the right thoughts into their minds, the power of these holy thoughts would shove the negative, false, sinful thoughts out.[2] I heard pastors shouting out "God loves you!" from the pulpit, as though the force of an elevated decibel level might drive the truth below the surface waters of the mind.

Counselor advice included repetition of Bible verses over and over for a month or putting these verses on 3"x 5" cards on a bathroom mirror as constant reminders—trying to jam new knowledge into the mind. As a counselor, I thought it was my job to be a storehouse of Bible verses, stress management strategies, addiction-breaking secrets, and other information that I could download into my patients' minds to make them well. Some of my patients knew the Bible better than I did, but they were hoping I could help them move the truth that they knew in their *heads* to their *hearts* and then into their *behavior.*

Similar to my New Age psychological training, there seemed to be an implicit belief that if a person could only grasp the correct knowledge in his or her mind, then healing would somehow happen. This is like receiving a diagnosis of having a malignant tumor in your body and believing that a cure will now magically occur because you correctly understand the diagnosis. But there is another step: the tumor must be removed.

We Christian counselors would enlist the Holy Spirit to give the blessing at the beginning of the counseling session, then relegate Him to the role of a silent bystander and witness. At the end of the session, we would call on Him to close the meeting.

I fell into this same pattern, even though I knew with my head knowledge that Holy Spirit was called Counselor, Healer, Comforter, and the Light who searches darkened regions of hearts to show truth-

---

[2] I do not discount the power of the Holy Spirit to penetrate deeply. To be discussed later.

fully what is going on there. Further, I knew that Holy Spirit is a Person who can communicate with us in any moment and bring to bear supernatural power to heal. But I was not communicating directly with Him.

Some change and healing occurred in me and in my patients, but it was more symptom-reduction than real healing. What would become clear later is the necessity to *remove* and *replace* dysfunctional beliefs, not try to shove them aside.

The truth was right there in Scripture. Jesus gave hints about removing the old and replacing it with the new, as in His image of putting new wine into new wine skins. He did not shove anything aside; He replaced it, made it new—a *new creation* (*2 Corinthians* 5:17). Wasn't the mission of Jesus to replace and exchange at the deepest levels of our being (*2 Corinthians* 5:21)? Like a transfusion. And didn't Jesus tell us that the Holy Spirit would be directly and personally involved in this exchange transfusion (*John* 16:13)? His truth was there in plain sight, but I didn't take hold of it and act on it.

A New Day

At this point in my discovery process, 1995, the story of Nancy in Chapter 1 enters the scene. It was a game-changer.

In my sessions with Nancy, the Holy Spirit had shifted me into the role of an assistant and facilitator, but I did not stay in that role for patients who came after Nancy. Rather than directly appealing to the Holy Spirit and trusting His guidance, I would occasionally suggest to patients that God had been with them in the dark, lonely places in their lives . . . and sometimes breakthroughs in healing would occur with this approach.

However, when there was any resistance to my suggestion, or when patients did not see, hear, or sense God's presence, I didn't know what to do next. Slowly I slipped back into my counselor role and continued to dole out advice. I began to read books on "inner healing" and "Spirit-led" ministry, but mostly remained a cognitive Christian counselor, sitting in the driver's seat of therapy sessions.

During this first decade of being a Christian, my old unstable, dysfunctional self was still in the driver's seat. I was allowing the Holy Spirit to have more dominance within my soul, but at best I considered God to be my co-pilot. My life was filled with turmoil, including the breakdown of another marriage, and becoming an every-other-weekend dad to two sons. My first son lived in California with his mother; visits were few and far-between.

My whole life felt torn apart and the pain seemed unbearable at times. My sense of belonging was shattered. Some healing began as I absorbed the Word and received Christian counseling, but a cavernous sinkhole opened up again inside my soul, only this time the hole felt deeper and the pain more acute.

In church after church, sermon after sermon, book after book, I heard the repeated message that God was a father who loved me, forgave me, and now accepted me as His son. But I had the same problem I witnessed in many of my patients, especially the men: I intellectually knew of God's love and acceptance in my head, but I didn't really believe or experience His love in my heart. I felt distraught, alone, and anxious.

About two years after the conclusion of therapy with Nancy, the parable of the talents kept coming to my attention in sermons and Scripture readings. The end of this parable about stewardship reads: "And cast the unprofitable servant into the outer darkness. There will be weeping and gnashing of teeth" (*Matthew* 25:30). Every time I read or heard that passage, I felt a niggling discomfort and would quickly turn my attention elsewhere.

One day, while sitting at my desk, I ran across the parable yet again and felt the same discomfort. This time I spoke inwardly to God: "Lord, please show me the truth about what I am feeling." This time I did not divert my attention away from the emotion. Immediately what emerged out of that murky feeling was a realization, a belief, that *I was that man in the outer darkness*. Then it was no longer a niggling discomfort I felt, it was abject fear.

I stayed in the experience, asking the Holy Spirit to guide me. I inquired why I was in the outer darkness, and a deeper belief came forward into my conscious mind: *I still believed that I belonged in the outer darkness because the amount of sin and evil I had done in the 20 years of my wayward, rebellious living was too much to be fully forgiven.*

Stunned by this inner script, I immediately challenged it with what I had read in the Bible and had learned during the past 12 years: In Jesus I was fully forgiven; He died for all my sins, past, present, and future; and His atonement means I have been reconciled with Him. However, none of these head-knowledge challenges had any effect on the anxiety and fear in my heart.

In the weeks that followed, I became painfully aware that I was unable to exchange my inner belief with the truths I cognitively knew. It felt like "the wall" between my head and my heart was firmly in place. Through counseling and coaching from a colleague, I realized two things: (1) these beliefs were entrenched remnants of twisted beliefs formed in childhood, and (2) my own performance-driven striving would be futile to resolve the issue.

During these weeks, I had memories of my mother telling me to "Be a good boy, Billy," just about every time I left the house as a child. Other memories surfaced, of catechism lessons about God's expectation that I could be good if I tried hard enough.

The inner agitation intensified, and I became increasingly desperate. One day while I was reading the Bible, I discovered these verses in *Ezekiel* 36:

> I will sprinkle clean water on you, and you will be clean; I will cleanse you of all your impurities and from all your idols. I will give you a new heart and put a new spirit within you; I will remove from you your heart of stone and give you a heart of flesh. And I will put my Spirit in you and move you to follow my decrees and be careful to keep my laws (*Ezekiel* 36:25-27 NIV).

Upon waking each morning, I prayed through those verses with my whole soul. My prayer became a simple, desperate plea for God to break open my hardened heart and replace it with a heart into which He could pour His Spirit.

Breakthrough

This went on for several weeks. Like the persistent friend who comes at midnight (*Luke* 11:5-9), I kept knocking and asking. I was calling out to God with everything I had. Then one day it happened. I was alone at home, lying prostrate on the floor, crying out to God. I had my Bible with me on the floor. In my mind's eye I saw the word *Galatians*. I opened the Bible to that epistle and felt inwardly directed to go to Chapter 4, not knowing what I would find there.

I began reading. When my eyes rested on verse 7, "You are no longer a slave but a son," that same personal Presence that had spoken to me in Brightmoor Tabernacle was speaking directly to me again: *You are my son, I have forgiven you.* Something in my heart painfully broke, shattered, released. Next, I felt a softening happen inside . . . and I felt a comforting love flow into my heart. Then a quiet peace.

The lie that I belonged in the outer darkness was blown apart and blown away, replaced by the powerful truth that I was accepted as a son and belonged in the Kingdom. In that moment, I was in God's presence, and I experienced being loved, Father to son. The darkness of fear dissipated.

The relief was incredible. I wept tears of joy. I read the next verse, ". . . and if a son, then an heir of God through Christ," and felt the truth of Jesus saying that He had come to set captives free (*Luke* 4:18). I felt free, I felt safe, and sensations of coming alive swept into my soul. I belonged. I was on the inside, no longer on the outside. A sense of peace came over me. It was new and it was uncanny, but I eagerly accepted what was happening.

Then I looked at verse 6, "And because you are sons, God has sent forth the Spirit of His Son into your hearts, crying out, 'Abba, Father!'" As depicted in those verses of *Ezekiel*, it felt as though God had removed my heart of stone and had given me a heart of flesh, into which He was pouring His Spirit.

Over the next weeks, I frequently returned to *Galatians* 4:7 to hear God whisper those words of truth and love. Tucked away inside of me were more lies and false interpretations of life experiences that would have to be discovered and removed, but this breakthrough was a beginning.

It now seems as though this event was a replacement "ritual" for the dedication ritual prayed over me when I was two weeks old. For decades I had lived with a priest-identity, then with no identity at all, mostly feeling isolated and lonely. Now I knew in my head, in my heart, and in my spirit, that I was a beloved son. I belonged.

Building on my experience in Brightmoor, this event was a significant deepening of my relationship with God. It was also a powerful therapeutic intervention in the treatment of my anxiety disorder. True heart healing had begun.

My conversion experience had for sure felt like dawn after a long night, but this current event felt (and still does) as though it was the first day of my life. It was the day I came to experience that I was a beloved son and that I had a father to whom I belonged. He was calling me to participate in His kingdom, in His family. I felt connected and attached, something I had never felt before in my life.

A truth settled into my heart: that the life of "I am life" is relational in nature. As a son, in relationship to God my Father, I felt alive. The sense of attachment and belonging was the deepest that I had ever experienced. It was like coming home.

Observations of an apprentice

1. The substance of "the wall" which I thought existed between head and heart was actually a lie buried in my mind. Somehow I had formed a belief which was contrary to the Biblical truth that God has forgiven *all* my sins in Christ Jesus. I believed that *I had gone over the limit in sinning and couldn't be fully forgiven*. Below the surface of my immediate consciousness, my mind had formed the understanding that my destiny was to be in the outer darkness.

Amazingly, this belief had the power to serve as a deflective shield, turning away thoughts of God's full forgiveness. The lie that *I had not been fully forgiven* was hidden somewhere in the recesses of my mind. Discovering that lie was like finding a secret dungeon in which a part of me was living in darkness, feeling like an outcast. God revealed that lie when I asked Him to show me what was going on. For sure there are more layers to the mind than the top layer.

2. Another awareness that broke through was that my full will was not available to make whole-hearted decisions. Since my profession of faith and full-immersion baptism in 1985, I had been in churches in which it was expected that, with the impartation of the Holy Spirit and the huge body of knowledge in Christian doctrine, a person *should* be transformed in spirit, heart, mind, and behavior. More than once I had heard sermons and counsel about how we *should* "get over it" or "put it behind you," referring to old beliefs and behavior.

I had stuffed my head with truths that contradicted the lies I held in my heart, but these embedded beliefs had been there for years and had formidable overriding power. I exerted much effort to *will* God's love down into that place in my heart, but I didn't have 100% of my will available to me. Unbeknown to me, part of my will was locked into the belief that *I was not forgiven*. The Holy Spirit showed me that lie. Then His truth, spoken right into the face of the lie, had the power to break its hold, as I gladly chose to receive His truth in place of the lie.

It was apparent that hidden beliefs were exerting their influence on how I felt and acted. I had somewhere, somehow unwittingly absorbed the lie that God wouldn't forgive me. When that belief came to the surface, I released it and then received God's truth recorded in *Galatians* 4:7, that *I was His son. I had been forgiven*. Truth was indeed setting me free.

3. It was the personal engagement with God that accomplished effective healing, not human-centered counseling. Healing and transformation happened through the intervention of God. He showed up directly through dialogue and personal involvement, not indirectly through an application of principles. In *Ezekiel* 36:25-27, God does every action: cleansing, giving a new heart, putting in a new spirit, removing the heart of stone, giving a heart of flesh into which He puts His Spirit, Who then moves the person to align with God's will.

I had experienced the truth of this Scripture, that God had done it all by *His* power. My co-laboring consisted of asking in faith; seeking for truth; being persistent; calling out with everything in me because I was desperate; ceasing from trying to do anything to fix the problem myself; and receiving all that the Lord offered.

Chapter 5
Exchanges For Life: Jesus Exchange Ministry

Over the next few years, I received much healing from the exchange of truth for distorted beliefs and interpretations of events that had lodged in my soul. Finally, the time came for healing the rejection wound I had carried for decades, since the 1960s when I left the seminary. The Holy Spirit brought into the open a buried belief I had formed as to why I had to leave. It was time to surgically remove a malignant growth in my soul.

In the year 2000, I had been invited to join the pastoral staff of the Fellowship of Christ, a church in Cary, North Carolina. A couple of years later, I had returned home from a retreat in which a discussion about my role in the church had gone awry, mostly because I had been triggered and swamped with feelings of being misunderstood. These feelings dropped me into thoughts and feelings of being isolated and alienated. I was immersed in a swirl of anxiety and extreme discomfort, yet I wanted to know the truth about the source of this turmoil. I requested an inner healing session from a colleague.

My ministry facilitator began by having me review and re-experience my emotions and thoughts as they emerged in the discussion with the pastors. Feelings of anger, rejection, and anxiety stood out. Surfacing from these feelings were thoughts of *not measuring up, not belonging*, and *being on the outside*. The feelings and thoughts were much stronger than what might have been generated by the discussion at the retreat, and my facilitator and I prayed to know their origin.

After a few moments, a memory emerged of a time in my late 20s when I was visiting my parents in Minnesota. One night I had mustered the courage to walk into my father's bedroom to ask him a question. The lights were dimmed and he was lying in bed winding down before drifting off to sleep. I had never heard an "I love you" from him, and I asked him what he thought of me. There had been an uncomfortable void in my heart for years and I hoped he might fill it in a satisfying way.

I can't even remember his reply when I asked him what he thought of me because it was so vague. I walked out of his bedroom deflated, emptier than before I entered, wishing I had not asked him the question.

In the ministry session, the pain from that memory flooded into my awareness and I prayed for further guidance: What did the Lord want me to know by bringing up this memory? Immediately, in my mind, I was transported into memories of my life in the seminary, strongly experiencing the beliefs that *I didn't measure up . . . I didn't have the right stuff . . . I didn't make the grade.* I had been a diligent student, salutatorian and valedictorian of my high school and college graduating classes, respectively, so I was surprised by this last belief about not making the grade.

Then something like a cellar trap door in my mind opened and the beliefs I had buried about why I left the seminary sprang out into the light of full consciousness. The beliefs: *God had decided I didn't have what it took to be in His elite corps of priests. I had been cut from the team. I wasn't good enough. I didn't come up to the grade-level of worthiness to be in the elite few He had chosen. He had taken away my vocation to be a priest. God had rejected me.*

Now all the buried pain, anger, and fear spilled out onto the center stage of my mind and heart. Even though the hurt had been stored in my heart for years, when it emerged it had a burning, searing energy as though it were a fresh wound. Sobbing, I held it all up to the Lord and asked Him what He wanted me to know about those beliefs.

Into my mind came large words, MINOR and MAJOR. The first eight years of seminary (high school and college) were called "minor seminary," and the last four years of theology training following college were called "major seminary." I saw that for many years I had believed that I wasn't good enough for the *major* league, that I was only good enough for the *minor* league, the minor seminary. I believed that I had been cut from the "A" team.

The Holy Spirit then beckoned me to release all these old beliefs to Him, along with the pain. I saw that Jesus had taken all those lies and pain upon Himself on the cross. For several sobbing moments, I did a full release. Then I felt a powerful pouring in of words and new feelings, filling and flooding the vacated places in my soul: *I had not been found unworthy. I had not been cut because I did not have the right stuff. God hadn't rejected me, He had released and liberated me so I could move on toward what He had in store for me. He has been preparing me for such a time as this, right here in North Carolina. The major seminary was not the major league. I am in His major league now because I am in what He has called me to. He loves me and He is equipping me. I may receive and accept that I have been called up to the majors.*

With great relief and tears of joy I allowed the Lord to make the exchange transfusion of His truth for the long-held lies. A comforting peace settled into every part of me that had previously been so distraught. I basked in the refreshing calm waters after so many years of harboring that rejection-belief and the pain it had wrought in me. The "cancer" had been removed and deep healing settled in. I felt immensely relieved and grateful.

Learning to assist the Master

The decade from 2004-2014 was a time of further healing and training. The field of Christian inner healing was broadening, deepening, and coming more in line with new discoveries, especially in brain science.

The left hemisphere of the brain is where reasoning, logic, and analysis take place. We store words and explanations here; it is like a reference library. The right hemisphere of the brain is non-verbal, imaginative, visual, and knows things by experiencing them. Interpretations, beliefs, and emotions are woven into experiences (memories) processed in the right hemisphere of the brain—the area that is accessed by inner healing methods.

In my counseling practice during the years after 2000, it seemed more and more futile to be shuffling around thoughts in the cognition-storehouse of the left brain or tinkering with behavior that was really coming from internal, negative beliefs from the brain's experiential knowledge base. By 2008, for those patients who were ready and could receive it, I functioned as a surgical assistant to the Master Surgeon who removed toxic "tumors" of lies and inaccurate interpretations of events. He then filled those places in the soul with His healing truths.

God continues to mold and shape whatever I hand over to Him. I have been a boy-destined-to-be-a-priest, a Catholic seminarian, a university theology instructor, a humanistic social worker, a transpersonal psychologist, a Christian counselor . . . and now a minister/therapist of inner healing, and a writer. Foremost, I am a husband, father, grandfather, and friend. I give all of this to the Lord, for Him to use as He will in accomplishing His purposes, because I know and experience my true identity: I am God's beloved son.

The process of Jesus Exchange Ministry

The replacement process of Jesus Exchange Ministry is one in which the person receiving ministry (recipient) can grow into what God *intends*, so facilitators begin each session in prayer, calling on His guidance from the beginning. We begin with *God-consciousness*, not *self-consciousness*.

In a typical session, after connecting with the Lord in prayer, what initiates the soul-search in a recipient is not a seemingly obvious trauma or painful incident that may stand out from hearing a person's biography. We call on the Holy Spirit to select: "Search me, O God, and know my heart . . . see if there is any wicked way in me" (*Psalms* 139:23). "Any wicked way" might be a recipient's sin, or it might be a wicked act that was done to the recipient, resulting in trauma pain. The primacy of the Holy Spirit inquiry over mind-analysis is a paramount first principle: "I, the Lord, search the heart" (*Jeremiah* 17:10).

In *Revelation* 3:20, Jesus says "Behold, I stand at the door and knock. If anyone hears My voice and opens the door, I will come in to him and dine with him, and he with Me." I know that there are various interpretations of this passage, but within inner healing ministry, the image is a depiction of this first step of seeking the Lord and opening up to receive His guidance.

When a memory or an incident in a recipient's life comes onto center stage of consciousness, we *invite* Jesus to be with us in that place. Jesus says He will "dine with him," i.e., bring the Bread of Life and the Water of Life—Himself—to minister to the person.

We do not conjure up anything, or "bring Jesus" into a picture or memory, or ask Him to do some action that we *think* would be beneficial. We ask what ministry the Lord wants to bring this day. As a facilitator, one is simply to ask the Holy Spirit to manifest how He wants to continue applying the Finished Work of Jesus Christ . . . in this moment, on this day, in this ministry session, for this willing recipient.

Not a counselor

A counselor is an advisor, a strategist, an analyzer, and a problem solver. A Christian counselor is expected to be a Biblical scholar and one who knows how to apply truths and principles found in the Bible and elsewhere. The minister of inner healing is a facilitator, not a counselor. One main difference between functioning as a counselor and a facilitator is the person sitting in the driver's seat in each process.

For years I was a Christian counselor firmly sitting in my pilot's chair, asking God, my co-pilot, to get us off the ground when beginning a session (opening prayer) and asking Him to bring us in for a smooth landing at the end.[3] It never dawned on me that the injunction "If we live in the Spirit, let us also walk in the Spirit" (*Galatians* 5:25) might pertain to walking through a counseling session in the Spirit.

God's heart and character are to heal. "I am the Lord, your healer" (*Exodus* 15:26 ESV). *Rapha* is one of His names. Rapha means to restore, to heal, to make whole again. People come for help because they are ravaged by sin and emotional pain. They need real healing and real transformation deep in their hearts—more than they need insight, advice, and strategies for stress-reduction.

It is God who "heals the brokenhearted and binds up their wounds" (*Psalms* 147:3); it is the Lord who is "near to the brokenhearted and saves the crushed spirit" (*Psalms* 34:18 NASB). He is the

---

[3] Several years ago, I actually pulled up behind a car with a bumper-sticker that read: "If God is your co-pilot, switch seats." In a phrase, this describes the role-shift for facilitating inner healing ministry.

Physician, the Surgeon, and the Counselor. The Lord has the compassion and power to heal. When I switched into the co-pilot's seat and began to facilitate direct encounters between a person and the Lord, His power and wisdom flowed into ministry sessions in unmistakable and effective ways.

His beauty for our ashes: facilitating the exchange

Living and walking in the Spirit also means listening in the Spirit. I spend much of my time during a session in a quiet interior dialogue of prayer with The Counselor—asking, listening, receiving, and moving with Him from step to step. Almost invariably, I find that the meanderings in and out of incidents and memories end up in a specific offer that the Lord has in mind for the recipient. The offer is often one of giving up an old belief in exchange for a truth that the Holy Spirit wants to impart.

In the Exchanges Diagram on the next page, I have depicted the interchanges of Jesus Exchange sessions. As facilitator I stay attuned to the Holy Spirit and wait for the invitation of the Lord to emerge in the dialogue. Lies, fear, shame, and sorrow will emerge from the shadows of the soul into the light. When this happens, the minister's role is to clarify the specific exchange that the Lord wants to conduct. A facilitator is still an assistant, but also a coach, pointing out what is targeted to be released, if the recipient is not able to discern clearly what is ready for exchange.

For example, an independent, self-sufficient part of a person emerges in a memory along with an embedded belief that *I have to take care of myself because no one else will.* When held up to the Lord in direct dialogue, the recipient senses or hears or receives an impression that the Lord is saying *I will take care of you.* Then the facilitator puts on his coach's hat and asks the person what he or she wants to do with what has been heard/realized/sensed. That old belief was placed there by choice or agreement and will be removed when a person is willing to give up the belief and receive the perspective that the Holy Spirit offers. Coming out of an old agreement and entering a new one.

DIVINE EXCHANGES
Our Father Reconciling us to Himself

> For He made Him who knew no sin to be sin for us, that we might become the righteousness of God in Him.
>
> 2 Cor. 5:21

RELEASE		RECEIVE
guilt, condemnation		full pardon
addiction		freedom, communion with God
fear		peace, trusting God
lies		truth that sets free
sorrow		comfort
pain		healing
shame		cleansing, sense of belonging
curses		blessings
troubled, anxious, agitated		calmed by His love
burdened		Jesus carrying our burdens
self-protection		The Lord my shield
bitterness, resentment, hate		forgiveness, compassion
self-will, stubbornness		humility, alignment with God's will
weakness		strength
impatience, desire to control		yielded to God
doubts		a believing heart
oppressed, despairing, defeated		freedom, hope, confidence

In the words under RELEASE in the diagram, I have listed just some of the many manifestations of our old self that Jesus brought down into death (*Romans* 6:6). Part of the coaching of a facilitator is to point out the recipient's option to release ungodly beliefs, shame, and other forms of darkness to the Lord Jesus. The Cross is a living symbol; it signifies Jesus drawing all wounds, curses, and sins unto Himself, for disposal.

The horizontal infinity sign in the diagram depicts the exchange-process within a healing session: As a recipient releases, say, shame to the Lord Jesus, the minister then facilitates the rest of the exchange—a recipient receives the inflowing truth and love from the Holy Spirit. In the case of shame, a person might receive a sense of belonging and/or cleansing as a replacement.

In the diagram, all three persons of the Godhead are involved in the actual exchange: The *heart* of the Father's love suffuses the whole scene . . . Love which is brought into our midst by Jesus through His self-sacrifice on the *cross* . . . and then Jesus' risen life is distributed into the time and space of our lives by the Holy Spirit, symbolized by the *dove*.

The invitation that occurs within a Jesus Exchange session is actually an invitation into the restorative exchanges of reconciliation and sanctification (*2 Corinthians* 5:18). The process is the Holy Spirit forming Christ's nature in a person—literally "Christ in you" (*Colossians* 1:27).

Jesus Exchange Ministry is about changing out old life and letting the Holy Spirit replace old life with new life. "New" means *His* life, *His* holiness, *His* love. It is a divine exchange transfusion.

Inner healing for all occasions

I want to say a few words about creating space and time in daily life for healing exchanges to take place. Inside the structure and steps of inner healing ministry is the simple relational reality of interacting with Jesus. The exchanges discussed throughout this chapter are elements of relationship: speaking and listening, knowing and being known, receiving love and loving in return. "Come to Me" (*Matthew*

11:28) and "Abide in Me" (*John* 15:4) are clear invitations for intimate relationship in which burdens can be released and His life can be received. In this relationship, the mission and intention of Jesus remains the same: to destroy the works of the devil, replacing them with His resurrected life.

When I engage the Lord during a quiet time in the morning, the purpose of quieting my mind is to receive an awareness of His presence. As I feel led, I open to a passage in the written Word and begin asking the Lord to connect me with Himself, the living Word, through the power of Holy Spirit. My desire is for Him to show me whatever He wishes me to focus on, and then to show me whatever He wants me to know about that place of focus. I seek communion with the Lord first, spirit to Spirit, giving permission for Him to then release His truth into my soul.

Sometimes inner healing moments occur during these prayer times as the Holy Spirit reveals some part of my old, dark self that has been hanging on. The release/receive dynamic takes place in these moments as I allow the Lord to make His exchange in my soul. And the same exchange can and does take place in moments during the day when an ugly or afflicted part of my soul shows its face. I don't always take the time for an exchange, but when I do, relief and peace follow. And however slowly, the relationship with my Lord grows.

I encourage you to go to the Lord directly when in distress, confusion, fear, or pain—like a child running to his father and mother—seeking guidance, reassurance, and truth. All the guidelines and steps I have given can be self-administered within your relationship with your Mentor, the Holy Spirit. The questions: "Lord, what do You want to show me here?" and "Holy Spirit, I don't know what to do here, what is your guidance?" can take you through many obstacles.

If you get stuck you can have a trusted inner healing facilitator, minister, or friend assist you in clearing away blockages. Some lies are deeply embedded in the soul and they don't easily relinquish their hold. A trained inner healing facilitator or a Spirit-led Christian counselor could be helpful in such a case. Also, new models of inner healing in groups and community settings have been developed. In the RESOURCES section in the back of the book, I suggest some inner healing ministries. Sometimes asking for help is the mindset of humility through which the Lord enters into the heart of the matter and provides healing.

Jesus Exchange Ministry in action

While looking over this diagram, a memory surfaced of a session I facilitated years ago. The person receiving ministry was a young woman who had to live overseas for an extended period of time because her parents were missionaries. She left behind her best friend, and the aching pain of this separation increased rather than abated as the months passed. She began manifesting symptoms of depression from the sorrow in her heart and had lost interest in daily activities.

As we approached the place in the healing session in which the recipient is encouraged to listen for how the Lord wants to minister, the image of Jesus on the cross came into her mind. It became clear that the Lord was inviting the young woman to release her sorrow to Him because He had already taken it upon Himself so many years ago.

Previously in her life, she had developed a trusting relationship with Jesus and responded now to His invitation by a willingness to release her sorrow to Him. After she did so, she began to receive a flood of love and comfort flowing into her heart, mind, and body. Some moments passed and she began to feel the companionship of the Lord Jesus right there with her, a closeness that was new and palpable. The image of Vine and branch grew vivid in her mind's eye, and she spent a few minutes soaking in the experience of abiding in Him, being grafted into Him, receiving Life from Him. The aching sorrow gradually ebbed away and was replaced with a comforting peace.

Months later I found out from her parents that her depression had lifted and she had resumed daily activities with her usual zest for life. It is likely that, in a new way, she was also experiencing Jesus as her steady companion and ever-abiding friend, maybe even her best friend.

Reclaiming inner healing

In the year 2000, I was commissioned to head up a counseling ministry within the aforementioned church, the Fellowship of Christ. A ministry team was formed to learn and facilitate what was called "inner healing." Because there was a wide spectrum of meanings for this term, we seriously considered scrapping the phrase altogether. Many New Age/New Spirituality counselors and therapists had adopted the term, imbuing it with multiple meanings. *Inner* might refer to Carl Jung's collective unconscious, reincarnation memories, or a spiritual realm in which angelic beings were "inner guides."

In the 1960s through the 1980s the term was taken up by several ministers of healing who Christianized it. These included Ruth Carter Stapleton, John and Paula Sandford, Francis MacNutt, David Seamands, and others. Through these ministers, the meanings for *inner healing* were greatly narrowed and defined by a Biblical understanding imparted to *soul* and *spirit*. However, controversy raged about whether "Christ-centered inner healing" was Biblically based ministry and therapy, or unscriptural "psychoheresy." The controversy continues today.

While deliberating about a name, our ministry team researched the word *inner* to see if it was found in the Bible. Our findings were surprising.

The finding that riveted our attention was learning that the stand-alone Hebrew word for "inner" most often referred to the temple. In Solomon's Temple, there were three courts: the outer court, the inner court, and the innermost (inner of inner) court. The latter was also referred to as the "Inner Sanctuary" or "the Most Holy Place"—the place where God dwelled (See *1 Kings* 6:16).

In the New Testament the meaning of temple went even deeper. *1 Corinthians* 3:16-17 NASB says, "Do you not know that you are a temple of God, and that the Spirit of God dwells in you? . . . For the temple of God is holy, and that is what you are." For the ministry team, the concept of a believer's body, soul, and spirit corresponded, respectively, to the outer court, inner court, and inner sanctuary of the temple.

Putting all of this together and praying over the matter, we realized that *inner* was a deeply meaningful Biblical word, and we wanted to reclaim it, not discard it. The healing that we believed we were called to was exactly this inner realm of soul and spirit in humans, whom we believed were created to be temples of God. Here in soul and spirit, humans were heartbroken, oppressed, and bound up in shame and fear. We knew and had experienced that God intended healing and restoration in this inner realm of human nature. And sometimes the beneficial effects of inner healing flowed into the body, the "outer court" of the temple.

From this point on, whenever you see the term *inner healing*, please understand that the explanation above is the context for the meaning I intend. For me, using the term *inner healing* is a way of taking back and reclaiming what was God-given in the first place.

Recipients tell their stories of healing

The following statements are verbatim quotes from recipients of Jesus Exchange Ministry. I asked recipients and patients to respond to these questions: Was your life changed in any way because of your facilitated sessions? Did any healing take place? If there were changes or healing, have they lasted? From your experience, would you recommend this approach to others?

The many testimonies that poured in from recipients provide confirming evidence of the Lord's intention to heal and restore our hearts:

"Inner healing ministry has taken me spiritually where Bible intake and traditional counseling simply could not. As a pastor, I whole-heartedly affirm the dire need for solid Bible teaching and other conventional spiritual disciplines, but I now see inner healing as an incredibly valuable aspect of the sanctification journey. Through inner healing, I have come to truly know God as Father, to recognize the voice of my Shepherd, and to appreciate more dearly the ministry of the Holy Spirit."

∞

"In memory after memory, God revealed Himself and His Truth against every lie I believed in those places. Life began to flow in. Light began to glimmer. There were more and more periods of peace and buoyancy in my life. Over time the periods of peace lasted longer, as God put the pieces of my soul back together. The truths that God revealed in those sessions have not left me eight years later."

∞

"It is likely that I would be in a mental hospital somewhere now but for the grace of Jesus and His inner healing of the lies I believed about myself and my life. He exchanged them for His truth about me, that I am his beloved and valued child and that He has a good plan for my life."

∞

"I had experienced several traumatic events during my life. But over the years I learned to repress the painful memories. In order to survive, I built a firewall around myself . . . . My memories will always be with me, but the way I experience them has changed. They no longer hold me hostage. My relationship with Jesus has changed completely since I have experienced inner healing. He no longer seems remote and abstract to me. He is my companion and my friend. I can feel his presence. He is the LIVING God."

∞

"What really blew me away about inner healing was that God speaks at all. I didn't believe in that, and I didn't trust most people who said they did. But I have no doubt that He spoke to me personally about me and it changed my relationship with Him and the way I practice my faith."

The many testimonies that poured in from recipients provide confirming evidence of the Lord's intention to heal and restore our hearts. I am grateful to those who took time to speak out. My apologies for leaving out some testimonies; it was a matter of space, not quality, that was the determining factor. Every testimony was inspiring.

PART II

DISCOVERING THE LARGER STORY

During many years of facilitating Jesus Exchange Ministry, I have experienced and witnessed major identity-shifts, outright expulsions of fear, shame-shackles broken off completely, and other manifestations of a God who is sometimes named Rapha—the God who heals. After completing *Healing Troubled Hearts* (2014), in which I recounted many stories of healing, it dawned on me that divine exchanges were not only descriptive of a healing ministry but were also descriptive of the whole process we call Christian sanctification.

My thinking broadened. I received a sense that the Lord was stretching me to consider that what He intended for human lives had a deeply transformative dimension. It became clear that the words of *2 Corinthians* 5:17 are not dramatic hyperbole: "Therefore, if anyone is in Christ, he is a new creation." The words speak a vivid sense of truth and life. A more expansive understanding of His plan broadened into seeing the interconnection of healing, wholeness, and holiness.

In this dawning awareness, a seed was planted that grew into my second book, *Becoming the Likeness of Jesus* (2018). What is sanctification other than being made one with Jesus Christ, so that His true human nature will flow into me as I stay grafted into Him, a branch in the Vine? Was this not what was happening in the Jesus Exchange Ministry? The ministry was a specific and effective way of gradually becoming the persons we were intended to be by becoming our true selves ... which takes place within our relationship with Jesus.

However, as soon as *Becoming the Likeness of Jesus* was published, I once again felt challenged and invited to explore more deeply God's intentions behind and through His Incarnation. I found myself struggling with Western traditional theologies about reconciliation and atonement. In so many Western theological analyses of the

Incarnation, the predominant focus was on the death of Jesus as an event of substitutionary atonement. The resurrection was presented as a separate event, sometimes almost seeming like an add-on, albeit an important one. However linked, the hyper-focus on the crucifixion seemed to present a semi-truncated Gospel. Significantly, Jesus always spoke of both the death and resurrection as the event that would happen when He went to Jerusalem.

Between the years 2018 and 2022, I was led to take a deep dive into the early Fathers of Christianity, those patriarchs whose writings have mostly been preserved and developed through Eastern Orthodox Christian theologians and historians. Two of these patriarchs are Athanasius and Irenaeus; both are major contributors to an expanded understanding of the Incarnation.

This research into the early Fathers has brought into sharper focus a realization that has been growing in me during the 25 years I have been facilitating inner healing sessions: The death and resurrection of Jesus are not separate and distinct events; they are inextricably intertwined as two halves of a whole. For me, it has been like looking at one of those plaques that have pieces of dark wood assembled together with pieces of light wood. If you look at the arrangement long enough, the word JESUS jumps into focus. Using this analogy, as I have kept the death (dark wood) linked together with the resurrection (light wood), the words and reality of *Redemption, Restoration*, and *Transformation* have jumped into focus.

The theology of the East keeps Jesus' death and resurrection together as a two-in-one event, and by so doing has opened up in me a deeper understanding of the Incarnation. So much is hidden and unimaginable until we hold Jesus' death and resurrection together as a unified reality, a seamless garment that in its wholeness reveals the Incarnation as redemptive, restorative, and transformative.

Many of the discoveries that are about to be presented are based on the inherent unity of Jesus' death and resurrection. I have found the Scripture-based discovery gems to be enlightening and enlivening. I hope such will be the case with you as you allow the dark and light pieces to remain linked as two phases of a single, and highly singular, event.

Chapter 6
God's Plan: Out with the Old, In with the New

> May Christ through your faith actually dwell, settle down, abide, make His permanent home in your hearts! May you be rooted deep in love and founded securely on love . . . . That you may really come to know practically through experience for yourselves the love of Christ, which far surpasses mere knowledge without experience; that you may be filled through all your being, unto all the fullness of God; that you may have the richest measure of the divine Presence, and become a body wholly filled and flooded with God Himself![4]
>
> (*Ephesians* 3:17-19 AMP)

It is clear from this passage that God's desire and intention are to indwell the innermost being and personality of humans. This is how He creates us anew, how He molds and shapes us into new creations. *Romans* 5:5 confirms this inflow of God's love: ". . . the love of God has been poured out in our hearts by the Holy Spirit who was given to us." However, as we shall discover, the old must be emptied out before the new is poured in to replace it. It is an exchange.

Not a personal growth model

Although the powerful passage from *Ephesians* above can at first glance appear to be a promo for self-improvement and self-devel-

---

[4] The purpose of using the Amplified Bible is to bring out the richness of the Hebrew and Greek languages. It goes beyond the traditional word-for-word concept of translation. The Amplified Bible gives other, clarifying meanings that may be concealed by the traditional translation method, while also giving the single English word equivalent for each key Hebrew and Greek word. For easier reading I have removed brackets and parentheses in the text.

opment, the opposite is true. God's masterpieces are not stand-alone works of art to be hung in a gallery. By coupling *Ephesians* 3:17-19 with *John* 7:37-38, we see that God's intention of filling us up with His love is so we can pour it out onto others. Becoming filled and flooded with the inwardly transforming love of Jesus has an outward, self-giving movement: "He who believes in [into] Me . . . out of his heart will flow rivers of living water" (*John* 7:38). Rivers of loving others.

Jesus' life and teaching were *against* self-realization. The entire character of Jesus is *self-expenditure*. Yes, God wants to fill us up until we are beautiful, plump grapes, but in becoming like Jesus, this means squeezing the juice out to nourish others. The nature of sin is the nature of self-realization, in that the basic belief undergirding self-realization is, *I am my own god*. I believe that this entrenched self-deification is mainly what has sealed the doom of the old life inherited from fallen Adam and Eve. The first principle in the Kingdom, above all, is that we worship nothing else in our lives but the one true God (*Exodus* 20:3).

Becoming like Jesus means that I allow the Holy Spirit to make me a new creation by redirecting and realigning my mind, heart, and will in ways that re-present (make present) Jesus' mind, heart, and will. In my own experience, as I reckon my old self to be dead and as I am slowly being formed into the likeness of Jesus, I more and more *desire* to serve others, to yield to love rather than selfishness. Let me express these thoughts with an illustration.

There is a story about a businessman who was a believer in Jesus. He and two of his associates were running through an airport to catch a plane. Delayed by unforeseen glitches in their business meeting in New York, the men were now hurrying to catch their flight back home to Chicago. As they turned a corner in the main terminal to head towards their gate, one of the men's briefcases hit a vendor's applecart. The jolt shook a large basket of apples on the cart, and they began to tumble onto the floor of the terminal. One of the men glanced back over his shoulder as they kept running. He saw a young woman come out from behind the cart, scurrying around to pick up her apples. The men continued running down the concourse to their gate. It was Friday afternoon and they very much wanted to make the flight and return home to their families.

They made it to the gate just in time! With sighs of relief and joking banter, they walked down the aisle of the plane to their seats. Two of the men took their seats in a row of three seats, the third stood hesitantly by the aisle seat. "What's up, Jack?" said one of the men who noticed a concerned expression on Jack's face.

"I'm going back," said Jack. "I'll see you guys in Chicago when I can catch another flight." He turned and darted out of the plane, just before the flight attendant closed the hatch for takeoff. With startled expressions on their faces, the men watched Jack exit.

Upon returning to the scene of the accident, Jack saw the young woman on her hands and knees on the cement floor, feeling around for the scattered apples. She was blind. A few travelers had returned some apples that had rolled out into foot-traffic, but most folks were moving swiftly to catch their flights.

The businessman bent down and gently told the woman that he was helping her gather her apples and replace them in her basket. She was weeping but nodded her head in grateful assent.

When all was set right, the man apologized to the blind woman, and taking her small hand in his, he placed into it a $100 bill, telling her that he was doing so. He said that she should buy a new batch of apples because many of them were probably bruised by the fall.

The woman, who had stopped crying because of the man's kindness, now began weeping tears of joy and relief. With her hand still holding the money and the man's hand, she turned her face up towards his and asked, "Mister, are you Jesus?"

I don't know what the man replied since the story ends with her question, but my response is *yes, she had encountered Jesus*. I know that the man could have been a non-believer and acted the same way, and that humans of no particular religious affiliation can engage in such acts of kindness, but the businessman was a Jesus believer. I want to make some observations to highlight the theme of being conformed to the likeness of Jesus:

- The man could have had a relationship with God whereby there was a level of personal communing sufficient for him to hear the still, small voice within, prompting him to act, per-

haps even prompting him to glance back over his shoulder while running down the concourse.
- The self-first proclivity in the man could have rationalized that the girl would probably be alright if he didn't go back to help her, but a sharpened moral capacity in him might have been strong enough to discern the right thing to do—and to do it by choosing to ignore his selfish inclination (die to it) and let his *will* engage with the call of Love.
- He laid down his life for another. He loved his neighbor as himself, to the point of putting her above his self-interest.

These three observations mirror characteristics of how I believe humans are made in God's image. We all want to hear those words, "Well done, good and faithful servant" (*Matthew* 25:21). I believe that this response will come not because anyone has completed a checklist of good actions, but because he or she has stepped into the personally transforming process of becoming the likeness of Jesus.

It could have been the very nature and life of Jesus flowing out from that man in the airport, like a river of living water, and the blind girl sensed *His* presence, *His* character. It's not much of a stretch to think that Jesus the Vine was there, acting through one of His branches.

Perhaps this story reflects a prophecy from long ago: "And out of their gloom and darkness the eyes of the blind shall see" (*Isaiah* 29:18 NASB). The young woman was able to "see" Jesus because of the man who *presenced* Jesus through himself . . . the Incarnation of Jesus Christ continuing through a member of His body here on earth (*1 Corinthians* 12:27). Jesus with skin on.

Jesus laid down His life that we might live; now we can lay down our lives that He might live through us. Isn't this the way of living that will touch our Father's heart, prompting Him to say, "Well done good and faithful servants, my true sons and daughters"?

The self: dead or alive?

In *Matthew* 16:24, Jesus says, "If anyone desires to come after

Me, let him deny himself and take up his cross [instrument of execution] and follow me. For whoever desires to save his life will lose it, and whoever loses his life for My sake will find it." A significant understanding of this passage is found in *Romans* 6:11, "Likewise you also, reckon yourselves to be dead indeed to sin, but alive to God in Christ Jesus our Lord."

Paul understood what Jesus was saying because the Holy Spirit had led him into the radical transformation of considering his old life to be dead, replaced by being a new creation in Christ Jesus. Throughout Paul's epistles, we find many references to the counterfeit human nature we inherited from the first Adam, a "nature" that was replaced by the authentic human nature of Jesus, "the last Adam" (*1 Corinthians* 15:45). We find words such as *the old man, the flesh, the old self*—all synonymous references to what we initially inherited.

What is the self? Is it not simply the unified activities of an individual human mind, emotions, and will within a physical body? The self is a dynamic core in which each person's character and conduct are shaped in specific ways.

Similar to the chambers of the physical heart, each individual self is a repository of whatever is poured into it. Then, like the heart, the contents are pumped out into the whole organism via thoughts, feelings, desires—all the way out into actions.

When we speak of *self*, we may indeed be speaking of what Jesus said in *Matthew* 12:34-35: "For out of the abundance of the heart the mouth speaks. A good man out of the good treasure of his heart brings forth good things, and an evil man out of the evil treasure brings forth evil things." In *Ezekiel* 36:26, God says "I will give you a new heart," to replace the old heart of stone. I am not necessarily equating *self* with *heart*, but they are similar in meaning.[5]

I am a person named Bill Day, created in God's image. Over many years, the formation of my self that has taken place within my mind, emotions, and will has been habitually bent inwardly towards

---

[5] It is beyond the scope of this book to attempt a lengthy or definitive statement of either self or heart. This brief description is my attempt to express what I understand to be the essence of self. Both self and heart are words that have many definitions attached to them in theology, psychology, and the arts.

egocentricity. This is a malformation that is beyond my capacity to unbend in the radical way that is warranted, in order to be an authentically loving, giving person. "Naturally," in my basic disposition, I am more self-seeking than others-centered.

Galatians 2:20 says, "I have been crucified with Christ; it is no longer I who live, but Christ lives in me." I believe that it is the *old self* that we are to die to, in agreement with God's decision regarding the fate of our wrongly developed, false human nature. My old thinking, feeling and acting system (self) dies in Christ, but there is still a *me*—a particular *person* created to be a son in the family of God.

When the Holy Spirit comes into a person, the exchange process of transformation is established (like carbon dioxide removal and oxygen replacement in the physical heart when we breathe). The Holy Spirit replaces wickedness and darkness with Jesus' capacity to love God instead of disrespecting Him, and to love one's neighbor instead of maligning him or her.

While we remain in Christ Jesus, the Holy Spirit creates everything anew— "a new creation." The God-created *self-structure* (mind, emotions, will) is not innately bad, needing annihilation so that we can live a supposedly *self-less* existence. We need to die to the false, self-absorbed, counterfeit human nature that is irremediably riddled with missing the mark (sin) of what God intended. However, we need a self in order to love, to give, to serve—to live out our lives the way God intended. We need a *new* self.

Jesus had a self. He speaks of "Myself" in *John* 5:30. Jesus used His human mind, emotions and will to love and care for those around Him. When I am drawn into Him, I become a Jesus-and-Bill self. "Christ living in me" is a hybrid. As I abide in Christ, the Holy Spirit recharges and re-aligns my spirit, and then re-aligns and reforms the mind, emotions, and will of the specific person that is *me*.

The reason I bring up the subject of *self* is that in many sectors of Christendom, a focus on *dying to self* has overshadowed the other half of the equation in *Romans* 6:11: "being alive to God." The word *sanctification* means to *set aside*. But sanctification in its positive sense means *set aside unto God:* "Now if we died with Christ, we believe that we shall also live with Him" (*Romans* 6:8). We can see from this verse that the second half of the exchange, after dying, is being filled with His enlivening life. We release the *old self* and, in Jesus, receive a *new self* so we can live a fully robust, joyful life. Jesus said He came that we "... may have life ... and have it more abundantly" (*John* 10:10).

Let us fix our eyes on Jesus to understand the blueprint. Jesus was completely dead to sin and yet able to be *in* the world without being *of* the world. He didn't cut Himself off from the world, He immersed Himself in it as light plunged into a vast darkness. Through constant communing with His Father, He was totally "alive to God." Wherever He went, love, light, and the joy of life radiated from Him in every direction.

Jesus poured out Himself in giving, caring, emptying out His life for others. He directed Himself inwardly towards communing with His Father, and outwardly towards serving, helping, encouraging, and laying down His life for others. This is the way of Jesus, and it is to be our way as well.

Far from *annihilating* our God-intended self, as suggested in teachings about *selfless* living, I believe Jesus wants to re-create the self of every person into the very image of Himself. It's *Genesis* 1:26 all over again: God breathing His life into our nostrils anew, and we become new creations, imbued with *new selves*.

Real transformation: the power of person-to-person interactions

During my childhood and youth, God seemed like a remote overseer who constantly evaluated and critiqued my performance. I felt that He was more likely to focus on what I had done wrong than on anything else. Later, my hidden belief that God had cut me from the elite squad of priest-trainees reinforced this image and kept me at arms' length from Him for many years. That image is in sharp contrast to now knowing Father, Lord Jesus, and Holy Spirit as three Persons who together love me dearly and are unreservedly poised to bring about the best for me in any given moment of my life.

When a man listens to the Living Word of God and hears Him

say that he is no longer a slave but a son, or when a patient hears Jesus tell her that she is not a loser but has a destiny of meaning and purpose, seismic shifts occur in those minds and hearts.

Jesus said that He is Truth (*John* 14:6). I have discovered that this doesn't mean He dispenses a storehouse of principles and concepts, like handing folks an operation manual and telling them to read it. In Person-to-person encounters, He is present through His words, His character, His heart.

For example, as a Christian counselor, I repeatedly told a patient that her sexual abuse at age four was not her fault. My words were helpful and soothing, but they did not have the power to swap out her false and oppressive sense of shame and guilt that would seep back into her soul after our therapy sessions. In a later session, however, after I had learned to facilitate Jesus Exchange Ministry, Jesus said to her, "It wasn't your fault." *His* personal power crushed and disposed of the lie that had been embedded in her soul for 40 years. Her shame shackles were broken (and stayed broken), and she felt free to be *a beloved child of God* for the first time in her life.

The experience of being loved by God is a core component of real change and transformation. I know and value the healing and nurturing that occurs when humans love one another, but I believe there is a *God-shaped void in every human heart* that only He can fill. Part of the freedom I now have is knowing Whose I am (realizing that I belong in God's family) and experiencing that God's love completes me and makes me whole, in a way that no human love can.

My relationship with God is the *foundational* place within which my life has been re-aligned in transformative ways. God can, and does, weave His will and His ways through a variety of loving human relationships here on earth; but however healing and nurturing my human relationships are, they are *supplemental*, not foundational.

Hence, in addition to my comments about old self/new self, there is one more introductory statement to be made before we dive into discoveries about transformation: **God, not human agency, transforms lives.** Often, even in Christian circles, the word "transformation" is used to convey changes or growth that, however substantial, are modifications wrought by human hands, by human strategies, by human engineering. No doubt significant changes can be made by human agency, but I have come to believe that true transformation is totally a God-action.

True transformation is synonymous with the radical nature of *exchange*; one thing is swapped out for another. When it comes to transforming fallen human beings, the radical remedy of exchange and replacement points to the extensive nature of our corruption, often a difficult reality to face. Only God can fix that condition and does so with an out-with-the-old-in-with-the-new remedy . . . Jesus. As we shall see, our condition was severe enough to warrant what might best be called a Divine Exchange Transfusion, otherwise known as the Incarnation.

With this introductory chapter of PART II in mind, the discovery process will now plunge into a Scriptural exploration of God's plan. If transformation is a main focus of God's plan, what is the *purpose* of God expending such huge resources of Himself to accomplish radical change in us? And how are Jesus' death and resurrection central features of this plan?

Let us fix our eyes on Jesus for He is the way, the truth, and the life. May He be the focus of all inquiry and discovery.

Chapter 7

Fixing Our Eyes Fully on Jesus

From shadow to reality

In the *Epistle to the Hebrews* 12:2, we are exhorted to "fix our eyes on Jesus," to focus on Him and Him alone. *Hebrews* 1:3 provides ample explanation for this focus: "He [Jesus] is the radiance of the glory of God and the exact imprint of His nature . . . ." All that God is, in His nature and character, is expressed perfectly by the incarnate Son.

The sun and its brightness form the image. The brightness radiating from the sun is the same nature as the sun. Though they are distinct, the brightness of the sun cannot be separated from the sun. "I and the Father are one," says Jesus (*John* 10:40). If there were no rays we could not see the sun, so also without Jesus Christ we cannot truly see God. It is in Jesus that God is revealed. So, going forward in this discovery process, looking unto Jesus will be the primary way of understanding what God has to say to us. Jesus is the living Word of God.

It has been said that every verse in the Bible points to Jesus. This thought expresses the understanding that all the Old Testament figures, events, laws, rituals, etc. are reflective indicators of the reality that is to come: the Son of God as the Messiah. Returning to the analogy of the sun, everything in the Bible is like the moon, which reflects the light of the sun.

Speaking for Himself on the matter, Jesus chastised the Sadducees with these words: "You search the Scriptures because you think that in them you have eternal life; it is these that bear witness of Me; and you are unwilling to come to Me so that you may have life" (*John* 5:39-40).

From the outset, I ask you to join me in fixing our eyes on Jesus, listening to Him to learn what God wants us to know about the very character and nature of God. On more than one occasion, Jesus challenged His listeners by saying, "You have heard it said to you . . . but I say to you . . . ."

Broadening the scope

My path of exploration has taken me on a journey to the East. From Augustine in the fifth century up to modern times, the Christian theology of the West has mostly camped out over the problem of sin, depicting Jesus as the Savior who can obtain for us forgiveness of sins, keep us out of hell, and provide a ticket to heaven, as per the scene I depicted in the INTRODUCTION. According to this view, the solution for the sin-problem is the cross. Once Jesus pays the supposed penalty price of death, the problem is fixed. Jesus then goes back to heaven and sends the Holy Spirit to spread the gospel of salvation.

For many decades of my life, this was the storyline I believed. In this view, the focal point is the problem of penalty, not the problem of sin-diseased human hearts.

In exploring early Church Fathers such as Athanasius and Irenaeus, a much broader picture of the Incarnation has stretched my mind, and indeed my heart, as I have realized more fully that the mission of Jesus goes far beyond the problem-solver Jesus I had internalized from childhood.

In absorbing the theology of the West (Augustine, Aquinas, Luther, Calvin, and others), my mind had been narrowed into a fix-it mode in which the *holiness* of God had become detached from the *relationship* dimension of our three-in-one God. The leading premise of this fix-it theory is that because God is holy, He *must* punish unholiness in a way that is commensurate with His perfect holiness . . . which means the penalty of death. There are Old Testament passages in *Deuteronomy* and *Leviticus* that seem to confirm this view.

"Commensurate punishment" has been construed by some systematic theologians to include the horrible torture Jesus endured as our substitute, reasoning that the extent of Jesus' suffering and torture is an appropriate punishment that matches the depth of our depravity. At a gut level that never felt right to me, but many theological books, articles, and sermons served up innumerable variations of this theory, and I accepted it intellectually as an essential doctrine of the Christian Faith. We will examine this matter in detail but let me begin with a few opening thoughts about a different perspective.

There is another Scriptural way of looking at the entire event of the Incarnation. From all eternity God has lived in a relational communion of love and fellowship between Father, Son, and Spirit. Creation is God's intention to have us participate in this fellowship. The Incarnation is a restoration of this fellowship. Jesus was sent ". . . so that . . . you may participate in the divine nature . . ." (*2 Peter* 1:4). To participate *again*. Paradise lost, Paradise regained . . . in Jesus.

Eastern Orthodox Christianity has lived and breathed this understanding for centuries. My exposure to this more expansive sense of the Incarnation, encompassing God's holiness *and* His love, has been instrumental for healing the division in my mind that had thought to detach God's *holiness* from His essential nature of *love*.

As will unfold in coming chapters, there are two arcs, a small one and a larger one. The smaller arc of the West extends from creation → to the fall → to the incarnation → to salvation from sin. The greater arc of the East stretches from union with God at creation → to the fall → to the incarnation → to salvation → to re-union with God. In this greater arc, human history is a shipwreck awaiting rescue, but the port of salvation is not the goal. The goal is for the restored ship to resume immediately its God-designed journey of union with God.

Irenaeus and other Eastern theologians regard salvation as the bestowal of a transformational process of renewal, in addition to the bestowal of forgiveness. To them, the question "What is salvation?" was clear: to be free from sin, corruption, and death in order to enter union with God once again. To be at one with God, as Jesus prayed (*John* 17:20-23).

In this view, freeing us from sin and death means dealing with the devil's dominion over mankind that has wreaked havoc and corruption in all human hearts. It means dealing not only with the *behaviors* of sin but also dealing with the evil thoughts and selfish intentions permeating our sin-prone fallen *hearts*.

For Irenaeus, the words of the Apostle John indicate the primary purpose of why Jesus came: "But the Son of God came to destroy the works of the devil" (*1 John* 3:8). Beyond forgiveness, Jesus was sent to destroy the evil that Satan had wrought by masterminding the perversity which had turned the souls of men and women into caricatures of what God had intended. Because of this work of the devil, the Incarnation becomes much more than simply the necessary prelude to Jesus making His way to the cross.

The discovery that has energized my soul and propelled me to make this major revision of my two previous publications is that Jesus' resurrection is part of His Finished Work. Funneling the Jesus-event almost exclusively onto the cross as the focal point eclipses the larger story.

As will be shown, Jesus absorbs our entire sin-prone counterfeit human nature into Himself (sponge-like) on the cross so that He can dispose of it, literally, once and for all, similar to draining out diseased blood in an exchange transfusion. However, that is only one-half of the event. The other half is the new life He was raised into after death, through His resurrection. He attained this life in Himself as Man in order to give it ("donor blood") to us as God. It is an exchange, a replacement, a transfusion.

There is a sense of wholeness in keeping Jesus' death and resurrection together as a single, seamless event. Hidden truths are revealed through this perspective. I hope to demonstrate that considering death and resurrection as two aspects of a single mystery will yield a more comprehensive understanding of who Jesus is, why He came, and who humans are and why we exist.

Chapter 8

Rescuing Us from the Miry Pit

For many years, the verses of the Bible that have literally given me shivers are *Luke* 4:16-21. Jesus had just returned from 40 days of fasting and prayer in the desert. He walked into the synagogue of Nazareth on the Sabbath day and was handed the scroll of the *Book of Isaiah*.

Standing up to read, He opened the scroll to Chapter 61 and read aloud:

> The Spirit of the LORD is upon Me,
> Because He has anointed Me
> To preach the gospel to the poor;
> He has sent Me to heal the brokenhearted,
> To proclaim liberty to the captives
> And recovery of sight to the blind,
> To set at liberty those who are oppressed;
> To proclaim the acceptable year of the LORD.

The part that always gets to me is after He handed the scroll back to the attendant, sat down, and everyone was looking at Him. Jesus said to them, "Today this Scripture is fulfilled in your hearing." He was saying that the "Me" of "The Spirit of the Lord is upon Me" was none other than Himself! Can you imagine sitting in that hushed synagogue when this event occurred and Jesus said that?!

These verses seem to describe a rescue operation to liberate and heal people who have been captured, enslaved, and broken. The oppression is such that the people cannot overcome it on their own, they need to be rescued. This sounds like the nation of Israel in their 400 years of captivity in Egypt. But these verses were written by Isaiah long after Israel had been physically liberated from Egypt. The Exodus had already taken place.

So, to what is "to proclaim liberty to the captives" referring? After Egypt, there had been other captors: Babylonians, Persians, Greeks, and at the time of Jesus the Roman Empire held the Jews in an iron grip. Was Jesus referring to a physical overthrow of Roman oppression, or perhaps another miraculous liberation like the first Exodus? Many of those who believed Jesus might be the Messiah expected this form of "liberty to the captives," and were disappointed when Jesus rejected this expectation.

Rescue from lie-infested minds and hearts

There was another view of captivity that was visible through many revelations of prophets such as Hosea, Ezekiel, Jeremiah, and by Isaiah himself through these verses read by Jesus in the synagogue. This was the captivity brought about by darkened minds and hearts resulting from the same mistrust of God exhibited by Adam and Eve. A pathway was laid down when our first parents believed the serpent's lie that God was holding out on them, that He didn't really have their best interests in mind.

Generations later, walking on this same pathway of distrust, the newly liberated Israelites complained about their provisions, to the point of wanting to return to Egypt. Eventually they also fell back into the idol-worship they had absorbed from Egypt's pagan culture. They believed the lie that God was holding out on them, that He wasn't to be trusted to take good care of them. Experiences of hardship in the desert caused the old lies to resurface: God is not good all the time, we have to take care of ourselves by our own means.

Here, in these beliefs, was the source of their real captivity; their minds and hearts became constricted with the fear emanating from what they believed about God. The prophets repeatedly spoke God's truth that He had carefully chosen these people and loved them with an everlasting love. He would never leave nor forsake them. He would be like a husband to them, and they were to be His beloved.

Many of the people chose to believe that these words were too good to be true. Their inner mistrust darkened their minds, blinding them from seeing truth. In their anticipation of what awful fate might befall them when God would eventually let them down, they became imprisoned by their own fear, letting a self-centered survival mentality be their captor.

Passover is a celebration of the miraculous and providential release from captivity of the nation Israel. But the Exodus was not a liberation from inner captivity, the darkened state of human hearts. Another "Exodus" would be needed, one that freed the Jewish nation, and indeed all people of the earth, from the *inner captivity* which has taken root through the grip of fear, guilt, and selfishness.

In Jewish history after the Exodus, this inner captivity manifested itself outwardly in exile after exile, captivity after captivity. Through the prophets, God spoke clearly that He loved them and wanted to be in a covenant relationship with them . . . and through them to reach out to the entire world. God repeatedly made impassioned pleas to the people to return to Him, like a pursuing lover pleading for His beloved to come home to Him. All to no avail.

What looks like an externally imposed punishment of oppression and captivity was actually the consequence of worshiping pagan idols and the self-centered living that results from living apart from God. As we shall see, God made us first and foremost for relationship with Him. Separating ourselves from this relationship by making something or someone else first and foremost is to break connection with the power of life itself. In addition, Israel had a special call from God that required a return to faithfulness, a return to God's ways. Oppression was a sobering and cleansing tool to refocus the nation that would bring forth a true healing for all nations.

Jesus the New Exodus

In the Roman occupation, during the time of Jesus, oppression was again gripping the people chosen by God to be the crucible of His plan for the whole world. And the same two layers of captivity (external and internal) were still in operation. In the external layer, Roman taxation was a crushing burden, as well as the many other constrictions of freedom the Romans imposed on the Jews every day. They were in bondage again. In the internal layer of captivity, raw pagan idolatry had been replaced by a religious system of laws and rituals, legalistically and harshly administered by the Pharisees and other religious leaders. It was a new form of idolatry, worshiping the letter of the Law rather than worshiping God. Jesus called out this form of inner oppression in *Matthew* 15:7-8:

> Hypocrites! Well did Isaiah prophesy about you, saying:
> 'These people draw near Me with their mouth,
> And honor Me with their lips,
> But their heart is far from Me . . . .'

A significant feature of this internal layer of captivity can be seen in the focus Jesus gave to the inner darkness of people rather than on the external captivity caused by the Roman occupation. In the Sermon on the Mount, in His interactions with the Pharisees, and in His many references to the Kingdom of God, Jesus clarified that "My kingdom is not of this world" (*John* 18:36). To Pilate He said, "You rightly say that I am a king. For this cause I was born, and for this cause I have come into the world, that I should bear witness to the truth" (*John* 18:37).

His kingdom was a kingdom in the spiritual realm, in which truth would become manifest, and actually be a liberating force: "And you shall know the truth, and the truth shall set you free" (*John* 8:32).

So, in quoting *Isaiah* 61, Jesus announces that from within this spiritual Kingdom of God in which the force of truth sets people free in their souls, He has been chosen and sent to bring freedom to earth. As such, Jesus is sometimes referred to as "the New Exodus." And in unambiguous terms, He brings the full picture of this rescue mission's operational strategy into sharp focus when He says, "I am the Way, I am the Truth, and I am the Life" (*John* 14:6 TPT).

The justice of God arrives in Jesus

In Jesus' ministry, it became increasingly clear that the truth setting humankind free would begin with acknowledging that in our separation from intimate fellowship with God, we have become spiritually poor, desperately needing the Gospel.

What is this Gospel? It is that Jesus Himself heals the brokenhearted, a brokenness resulting from our inner separation from God. Jesus Himself brings liberty to us who are captives of our confining self-centeredness. He Himself is the Light of the world (*John* 8:12) in Whom we who are blind can recover our inner sight and see the truth that will set us free. Finally, Jesus Himself frees those who are oppressed by the fear and anxiety emanating from not trusting God.

Boldly and with authority, Jesus spoke aloud to the Jewish listeners in the synagogue of His hometown, Nazareth, and He speaks these same words to us today: He is the One who has been sent to heal, to set free, to set aright all that is so discombobulated in our wounded hearts and darkened minds.

Finally, in verse 19 of *Luke* 4, we see an amazing proclamation that powerfully accentuates His mission statement of healing, freedom, and restoration. Jesus says that He has ushered in "the acceptable year of the Lord." This is a reference to the Year of Jubilee, each 50th year of the Jewish calendar in which all debts were forgiven, and things returned to the way they were at the beginning of the cycle of 7x7 years.

In effect, Jesus announced that His arrival on the scene signals the turning point of time in human history, a time in which all created things, beginning with humans, will be restored to their original design and condition. This design is what was established in the mind and heart of God before time began. As such, the assignment given to the Son of God is not only a rescue operation to free enslaved humans from captivity, but it is also a mission to re-establish the Kingdom of God upon earth. This mission is a reclaiming, a restoration, a definitive *return of what God intended from the beginning.*

In the larger story, God's story, each 50-year Jubilee is a small-story enactment and reminder of the total restoration and return of God's justice. In Hebrew, *justice* is the return of God's original design for His creation. "At the end of the day," as the cliché goes, God will have His way. He will rescue and restore His creation and eliminate everything that is not part of His design. He has already done so in Jesus and is doing so in those who immerse themselves in Him.

I have come to believe that, indeed, Jesus is God's Jubilee.

Chapter 9

Reclaiming What Had Been Stolen

There was a time when the earth, humanity, indeed the universe, did not exist. Creation was an act of a Creator we call God, but what is distinctive about the Christian view of God? I believe a first distinction is the doctrine of the *Trinity*, and a second is the *humility* of God.

The Bible tells us that the Father loves the Son, the Son loves the Father, and they share all things in love and fellowship with the Spirit. To believe in the Trinity is to believe that God is a relational Being. It is a belief that relationship, fellowship, self-giving, and other-centeredness are core characteristics of God.

The second distinctive feature of the Christian view of God is humility. Unlike the pagan gods of the Old Testament who were distant and preoccupied with themselves, the Christian God is preoccupied with *us*. From before the foundation of the world, *Ephesians* 1:4-5 tells us that God had an amazing plan to draw us near to Himself so we could participate in the circle of loving fellowship that has eternally existed in the relationships of the Trinity.

Is it not amazing that "Then God said, 'Let Us make mankind in Our image, according to Our likeness'" (*Genesis* 1:26 NASB)? Equally astonishing are the words, "Then the Lord God formed the man of dust from the ground and breathed into his nostrils the breath of life; and the man became a living person" (*Genesis* 2:7 NASB).

It looks very much as though God wanted to give *Himself* to us, so that we could be filled to overflowing with His divine life. This superabundant life points to a major reason Jesus said He came: "I have come that they may have life, and have it to the full" (*John* 10:10 NIV). Moreover, throughout the Bible, it is repeatedly revealed that God was and is determined to make sure we have this fullness of life . . . even if it means stooping down, crossing the chasm between Creator and creature, and lifting us up so we can share in everything He is and has.

From belonging to separation anxiety

The Genesis narrative indicates that God entrusted the care of the earth to Adam and Eve, and in turn they were to trust that He, their Creator, would take care of them. A covenant of trust. How powerful *trust* is in a relationship! Imagine you are in a healthy, loving marriage. Now imagine a neighbor coming to you, telling you that your spouse is having an affair. The neighbor seems genuine and shows you digitally-altered photos of your spouse in the arms of another person. Even though your spouse has been faithful and there is no truth in the accusation, you succumb to the temptation and believe the lie. Immediately something within *you* changes. You feel cut off from your spouse, who in a moment has become an untrustworthy enemy, not a friend. Fear rushes in. You pull into yourself, no longer believing that your spouse has your best interests in mind. You shift into a belief that you have to take care of yourself.

Something similar to this scenario is what I believe happened in that first garden. Jesus tells us that Satan is the father of lies and that he has been a liar from the beginning (*John* 8:44). The serpent told Eve that God was holding out on them, that He didn't have their best interests in mind. Satan lied about the goodness, faithfulness, and deep love God had for our first parents. The Fall happened when they believed the lie. The circle of love and trust was broken in their hearts and minds, and fear rushed in, along with a withdrawal into themselves.

A survival-self would naturally form in their hearts, based on the fear that they could no longer trust God to take care of them, so they would have to take care of themselves. Further, in their fearful minds, doubts could easily arise: Who knows other ways God might be untrustworthy? There they were, with fear, self-centeredness, and doubt—the unholy trinity of consequences that take root in the heart when lies are believed, when trust is shattered, and the circle of love is broken.

In the *Genesis* narrative, we have a picture of humankind breaking from a stress-free relationship of trust, and falling into a self-centered, anxious state of mind, fending for themselves in drive-to-survive mode. "I have to take care of myself," and "I'll do things my way" became governing guidelines by which to live. Out on their own, they and their progeny had to learn to cope with life outside the harmony of their relationship with God.

They became survivors of trauma, even though the trauma was self-inflicted by the choice not to trust what God had said. God did not abandon Adam and Eve, nor humanity; they broke the attachment bond by breaking the covenant of trust. I believe that breaking trust with God was a traumatic blow, resulting in what I call the *Separation Anxiety Disorder of Humankind*. A difficult chapter began for humanity. It is a chapter that continues to this day.

In my experience, the most disturbing consequence of living in the grip of this separation anxiety disorder is the loss of a sense of belonging. When I believed God had rejected me as unworthy and unfit to be a priest, a vocation I believed was my identity, I wandered the globe aimlessly for decades with no sense of who I was or where I belonged. I was anxious, angry, and insecure, trying to find my true identity.

In the first section of this book, *A STORY OF SEARCHING FOR HEALING AND TRUTH*, I chronicle the desperate, dysfunctional decisions I made in search of a sense of belonging. Adam and Eve initially had this sense of belonging to God, not as property but as relationally bound to Him by love. He cherished them. Knowing that they belonged to Him and that He delighted in them must have bathed their souls in peace and security. Losing that sense of belonging would have ushered in anxiety and insecurity.

> *At this point in my life, I consider a sense of belonging to be perhaps our greatest basic human need.*

Jesus brings back a sense of belonging

A deep sense of belonging was lost when these two "branches" became separated from their "God-vine," and began to scratch out life on their own. God didn't abandon Adam and Eve; the prophets of the Bible give passionate voice to God's continual pursuit of His children. But human mistrust of God has grown with each generation, leading up to our current times in which this mistrust has become a driving force of expelling God from entire cultures.

With this in mind, I believe that the reclaiming mission of Jesus was, and is, uppermost in God's heart. He knows in His own saddened heart the awful pain humans experience as they descend into distorted senses of identity when apart from Him. And He too feels distraught at the loss, for in His heart He passionately desires union with us. The plea of Jesus in *John* 17:21 illustrates this deep desire: "... that they all may be one, as You, Father, are in Me, and I in You; that they also may be one in Us . . . ."

What comes to mind as I write these words is the picture of the prodigal son's father running out to meet his returning son, while his son was still a long way off (*Luke* 15:20). The father's heart of compassion prompted him to run joyfully to welcome his son home. Through Christ Jesus, God our Father comes directly to us, inviting us back into intimate relationship with Him.

Sent to reclaim what humankind and God had lost

In tracking the degradation of mankind's original status as created in God's image and likeness, the Biblical depiction of our condition after the Fall is dire indeed. The human race descended into the darkness of its own mistrust and doubts about the character of God. In continuing to believe the lie of the evil one, children of Adam and Eve became blind to a true perception of God and of themselves.

God remained God, the same as always—steadfast, long-suffering, and merciful. What changed was the Adamic line of humans, generation after generation. Each person projected his/her fear and anxiety onto God, creating a mythological deity that wasn't really God (We do the same today).

Slipping more and more out of mankind's consciousness was remembrance of God's heart of love and goodness. Humans turned from worshiping God to worshiping mythological gods of their own imagination, which might be anything within the created order: fire, water, money, sex, power (See *Romans*, Chapter 1).

The problem to observe here is that worshiping false gods isn't just "doing wrong things." Distortion and misperception take hold in one's entire self, twisting and perverting the soul. This process is the formation and congealing of the *false self*. The human soul becoming ever more diseased with the cancer of selfishness.

Worse, to whatever idol we give our worship (make the top priority in our lives), we also give over our power and authority. The etymology of the word *addiction* is revealing; it is similar to what we mean by *worship*. Addiction means to *sign over to, to surrender to*. It connotes a dynamic in which one places oneself into a servant/master relationship, agreeing to do the bidding of the power to which one surrenders.

Who is the master of our addictions? Satan, the arch-narcissist himself. When addicted, we fall under his control, we belong to him. The basis of his hold on everyone in the Adamic bloodline is the alignment of our souls with his basic disposition of self-centeredness. We are all narcissists. The prison cell is our own false self, the old fallen self. It is the survivor self, living in isolation, living apart from the only surrender we are designed for: the humble yielding of ourselves to communion with God.

As Alcoholics Anonymous has so wisely stated it in Step One of their protocol: "We admitted we were powerless . . . that our lives had become unmanageable." The problem that I have found to be the most entrenched and difficult in my life, and in the lives of many patients and friends I have known, is how to become free from this addictive captivity, this prison of the false self.

> *Because it is so essential to real freedom, I have concluded that the way out of this captivity is the most consequential passage in our human journey here on earth.*

Who among humankind could and would see the truth about God's character? Who could and would stay in trusting relationship with Father God and know His character as faithful and true? Who could overcome the selfishness of survival-self living and turn humanity back to its divine design of self-giving? Who could overcome the false projections onto God that stemmed from the deep shame, fear, and loss of a sense of identity? For just such a soul transformation would be needed to undo the tragic destruction of God's intended destiny for humans, a destiny to live out what it means to be human beings who actually reflect God . . . humans restored to *imago Dei*, the image of God in human form.

Up to the time of Jesus, a real liberation from the captivity of human souls had not taken place. A real Exodus was needed, a radically new and different Exodus for the millions of human souls locked into a seemingly hopeless condition of slavery, the slavery of a false, counterfeit self. This was the human condition of everyone when Jesus arrived on the scene. All humans were living with Stage Four soul cancer, in the merciless grip of the master and god of this world, the devil.

Dealing with a robber

"The reason the Son of God appeared was to destroy the devil's work" (*1 John* 3:8 NIV). These inspired words of the Apostle John are often overlooked, or insufficiently explained in systematic theology's assertions about the reasons for the Incarnation. What is the devil's work? He lures us to keep turning to our own ways rather than trusting God. His foothold in our minds seduces us into intellectual errors about God's character and our identity. He blinds us from seeing and believing that the Gospel is an invitation to be reconciled with God through a relationship with Jesus Christ. He is the narcissist master of enslaved humanity and was three times referred to by Jesus as "the ruler of this world" (*John* 12:31; 14:30; 16:11). *1 John* 5:19 tells us ". . . that the whole world lies in the power of the evil one."

In the first three centuries after the time of Jesus, commentaries on Scripture coming from the early Fathers of the Church are replete with portrayals of the devil as a rebel and a robber, a usurper of God's authority as Creator of all.

In the second century, we find this theme robustly dealt with in the writings of Irenaeus, a Greek bishop recognized both by the Christian Church in the West and the East. In his doctrine of *recapitulation*, Irenaeus saw the need not only to overthrow the usurped authority of

Satan, but he also clearly saw the mission of Jesus as rebuilding and healing humanity within Himself. Recapitulation simply means that everything the first Adam did wrong, the second Adam did right, thus reversing in Himself the destructive damage Satan had done to human nature. Jesus restored human nature to its original design of being the *imago Dei*, the image of God.

Another Father, Justin Martyr (A.D. 103-165) taught that Christ came not only to defeat death and overpower Satan, but also to restore humanity back to God's design, thereby re-establishing God's intention for us to partake of eternal life with Him.

However, in the fourth century, the Roman emperor, Constantine, began to merge the Christian Church with the Roman Empire. The Church in the West became suffused with the whole Roman legal system. Imposed imperial laws became intertwined with Christian theology, and an entire judicial system mixing church and state developed. This system focused on penalty consequences for infractions of the law, and it crept into Christian theology, gradually replacing a restorative understanding of the Gospel with a focus on punishment.

The Church in the West veered off in this direction of meshing church doctrine with civil law. Such a veering produced such fruit as the Crusades and the Inquisition, in which heretics, apostates and infidels were "felons" deserving the penalties of torture and death.

Fortunately, the Biblical understanding of restoration and soul transformation took root and was preserved in the Eastern Orthodox Church. But an inevitable split came in 1054 A.D. when the Great Schism of the Greek East and Latin West took place. East and West would go their separate ways for centuries, challenging individual believers to seek and discover wellsprings of truth in each theology.

I grew up in the Latin (Roman Catholic and then Protestant) West, but in the past few years the Biblical themes of restoration and transformation have flowed into my soul through deliberate exposure to theologians of Eastern Orthodox Christianity. It has been a discovery of the Biblical threads of *rescue, reclaiming, redemption, restoration, recreation*—all pointing to a *return* of what both God and humankind lost. This discovery has gripped my soul, producing an enhanced understanding of the Gospel and a greater depth of intimacy with God.

In the next chapter, I enter the heart of this discovery project: the mission of Jesus to *redeem* mankind. The Son of God was sent to rescue and reclaim fallen humanity, but how could real reclamation of God's original design be accomplished, given the deep soul blindness and soul slavery of the human condition? If God's intention is to have us partake of His very life, to have us return to union with Him, how could this be, for He is holy and we are pervasively unholy? He is Holy Love and we became unholy selfishness. These two states are in direct opposition to one another.

It is a problem of cosmic proportions because, as indicated by the inspired writings of Paul to the Romans, Ephesians, and Colossians, what happens within humanity affects all creation. This problem is indeed *a divine dilemma.*

Chapter 10
The Divine Dilemma

There is a story about a man sitting at the defendant's table in a courtroom, waiting to hear his sentence from the presiding judge. The man had been found guilty of sexual assault, armed robbery, and murder. In a solemn voice the judge announces, "John Doe, you have been found guilty on all charges, and are hereby sentenced to the penalty of death." A subdued gasp waves through the crowd of those attending. After a long pause, the judge continues, "But someone has volunteered to pay the penalty for you. He will die in your place. You are free to go." The surprised and greatly relieved man thanks the judge and quickly leaves the courtroom. The backstory is then provided: The volunteer substitute taking the guilty man's death penalty is actually the son of the judge. The story ends by revealing that it is an analogy of what Jesus did in paying the penalty that we had been given and so richly deserved.

At one time in my life, my inner response when hearing this story was gratitude, realizing that along with everyone else, I was "John Doe." However, in the past 25 years my mind has inquired about the rest of the story. What was the freed man likely to do after leaving the courtroom? I had heard sermons about the overwhelming gratitude a person would feel in acknowledging the magnitude of Jesus dying in their place. This realization would be (or should be) sufficient to motivate a person to make a change of heart as well as changes of behavior. Transformation by gratitude.

Now, when I tell this story while preaching, I ask the congregation to answer the question of what the freed man will do after he leaves the courtroom. Sometimes folks will offer, aloud, "He'll go back to his old way of life." Almost certainly. Why? Because the gratitude of a self-centered human may last for hours, days, or even weeks, but it will fade. It won't be a transformative force. His habituated selfishness will return and take over.

In itself, forgiveness does not produce transformation. The man's sinful and illegal acts of sexual assault, robbery, and murder are far more than violations of God's laws and human laws that can be erased through pardon and forgiveness. These acts are *symptoms* of pathological soul disease.

The "freed" man is neither free nor liberated. He is similar to the Israelites who were physically liberated from slavery in Egypt but carried within their hearts the doubts and mistrust of God that had cultivated self-centeredness in their fallen souls for generations. The man walked out of the courtroom with his inner addiction to self still keeping his soul in prison: ". . . an evil man out of the evil treasure of his heart brings forth evil" (the words of Jesus in *Luke* 6:45). Why wouldn't he fall back into the habitual selfish heart and mind he had developed for decades?

What if, in the story, the judge was actually the defendant's real father? What if the healing and restoration of his son's wicked heart mattered to the judge just as much as satisfying the requirements of justice? What if the word "justice" meant the broader Hebrew sense of setting things right, the way they were originally? What if justice meant restoration? The story of the convicted man might follow a different direction. Let's do a "Take two" with a second version of the story.

The judge might say something like, "John Doe, you have been sentenced to death but there is something you don't know." Having said this, the judge takes off his black robe, steps down from his bench, and stands in front of the defendant. A younger man steps out from a side room and stands next to the judge. They both look with kindness at the convicted criminal. The judge proceeds to tell the man that he is actually a long-lost son of his, and that the man next to him is his brother.

Together, the father and son invite the man to come home with them and live in their home, where they will be joined by another family member who has many powerful skills of healing and rehabilitation. The truth is, they soberly tell the man, he has a terminal soul disease and will indeed die if he continues to live as he has lived, that is, a life of rebellion, greed, violence, and lusts of all sorts. They tell the man that they can expunge this disease of selfishness from his soul and turn his heart around, from being a *grabber* to a *giver*. It will be a long process, but they will stay committed to him for as long as it takes.

They tell him that such a turn-around will enable him to live a full, healthy, joyful life. He only needs to accept that the dire news they are telling him about himself is true, and to accept their offer. They will do the rest. They will set in motion the entire process of healing and rehabilitation. There may be consequences of reparation for the damage he has caused, but they will help him through all of those as well. They will never leave nor forsake him. This new life is what they offer as a way out of what would surely be a journey to death.

The son standing next to the father steps closer to the wayward son and looks deeply into his eyes, telling him that he will be an integral part of the rehabilitation. He says that he himself has already overcome the diseased condition of the man by laying down his own life. He will explain later. Then he puts his hand on the stunned and astonished man's shoulder, telling him that if he accepts their invitation, the two of them will spend much time together and become good friends. The father and son end by telling the man that he belongs with them, that he has been lost but has been found. "Come home," they say in unison.

In addition to not finding solid Scriptural evidence, one reason I no longer believe in a penalty-substitution theory of the Gospel is because, as can be seen in the first version of the story, it doesn't deal with the old self. The selfish orientation of humankind that has embedded itself into the spirits, souls, and bodies of humans since the Fall is not touched at all by this theory. When the man in the courtroom is set free because a substitute is punished in his place, nothing changes in the man's heart. It is a mere legal acquittal. The only thing that happens is that someone is punished, and it is then declared that the demands of justice have been satisfied.

In the second version of the story, the behavioral actions (sins/crimes) *and the heart* from which the crimes flowed are addressed. It is a restorative understanding of the Gospel, and the healing offered is a kind of relational rehabilitation in which the mission of Jesus steps forward boldly: "... It is not those who are healthy who need a physician, but those who are sick; I did not come to call the righteous, but sinners" (*Mark* 2:17 NASB). And all of us are the sinners who are sick!

I believe the second version of the story more accurately describes what we find in the four gospels and in Paul's epistles. As we will track, the invitation of the judge and his son is an invitation to immerse ourselves into totally new relationships with Father, Jesus, and Holy Spirit, offering a way out of spiritual death into eternal life. It is a model that for me is true to God's nature as described by the words: *holy love*. Let's have a look at these two words.

The dilemma

The Bible tells us that God is holy, forgiving, merciful, and just, among other attributes. All these attributes, like facets in a diamond, are radiant windows into the heart of God. But Scripture does not say that God is holiness, is forgiveness, is mercy, or is justice. When it comes to love, however, there is a difference. *1 John* 4:8 proclaims that "God is love." God does not merely act out love, He embodies it. Love is His core, His essence. *1 Corinthians* 13:4-7 NIV tells us that love is not self-seeking; it is other-centered, self-giving, sacrificially giving for the benefit of others, thinks no evil, and stands in truth. God is the boundless, eternal reality of goodness and love out of which the cosmos is built. God is everything we mean by *agape* love: a perfectly self-giving, other-centered kind of love.

From this perspective, the reality of love can be seen as the underlying law from which flows a constant giving of Himself to uphold and sustain the universe. This self-giving love is the design and order by which all creation was constructed to operate. Simply put, the Law of Love is the Law of Life. Harmony with this principle of love brings life, health, and happiness. Disharmony results in pain, suffering, and death. Jesus sums it all up pointedly in *Matthew* 22:37-40 when He states that love (of God and neighbor) contains everything in "all the Law and the Prophets."

The law of love operates like a circle, a current that flows throughout everything God creates. In each breath, we demonstrate this circle of giving: We give out carbon dioxide to the plants and the plants give back oxygen to us. We can see this law of love all around us in nature: The oceans give their water to the clouds, which rain down and give water to plants and animals. Lakes and rivers are formed by the rain, ultimately giving back to the oceans to start the circle again. We speak of "the circle of love" and that "what goes 'round comes 'round." Or, maybe better, what goes out from you will return to you in some form; what you sow, that also you will reap. Each day we live either in circles of harmony or disharmony with the law of love, the law of life.

Self-giving keeps the circle of giving and receiving going; self-grasping breaks the circle and ends in death . . . like the Dead Sea which receives from the Jordan River but doesn't give out in any way. It keeps everything to itself, and so names itself.

When God breathed His life into Adam's nostrils (*Genesis* 2:7), creating him in His image and likeness, He breathed into him a kind of spiritual DNA that was loaded with all the features of this self-giving, other-centered dynamic.

On the level of human relationships, one thread we are tracking here is what happens when the circle of love is broken. When trust is broken, disharmony results. The entire history of humankind can be summed up by acknowledging the disastrous disharmony that occurred when people believed lies about God. Instead of following the self-giving principle of Adam's hardwiring, which would be giving back love to God through trust and obedience, Adam and Eve believed the serpent's lies.

Our foreparents shifted into self-seeking rather than self-giving, thereby breaking the circle of love. All the pain, greed, suffering, broken dreams, violence, and death that this world has known are expressions of the misalignment with the law of love that has cascaded down through the centuries from what was set in motion at the Fall.

This disharmony has flowed through humans into all the institutions and cultures of human endeavors on this planet. All creation was affected by the Fall, but around us in nature we can still experience the harmony of giving and receiving. The law of love is visible in nature. But within humanity we see a predominance of disoriented disharmony, the law of love operating much more sporadically and inconsistently.

Now, regarding the *holy* part of *holy love*. Because Adam and Eve were created in God's image, they were hardwired for faithfulness and trust. They must have felt discordancy in their souls because they had broken the love circle through their self-seeking choices. Something changed in them. They hid. They felt shame and guilt. What would have happened had they gone to the Lord in open transparency, acknowledging that they had messed up badly, rather than defensively going into blame-shifting mode? "It was the woman You gave me"; "It was the serpent."

We don't know the answer to that question, but if we look at the whole history of Israel's sojourn, we see God in constant pursuit, trying to woo humans back to Him. But the inclination to self-survival (based on doubts and fear of God) kept the Israelites, and indeed all mankind, in continual blindness about God's true character.

When we say that "God is holy," the portrayal of God sometimes carries the projections we have put upon Him from our fallenness. From feelings of guilt, shame, and fear, we create a god in our imaginations who "must be" disappointed, displeased, and poised for retribution. As it has been said: "God created us in His own image and likeness, and we have been returning the favor ever since!" Not truly knowing God, we create Him in our likeness.

Much of the penal substitutionary theory (It is important to know that it is a theory, not orthodox Christian doctrine.) is based on a medieval sense of God as a monarch, a king on His throne, a solitary potentate whose honor would be grossly offended by sin because He is so holy. "Somebody has to pay" goes the refrain. When a king was offended, honor and holiness "demanded" that the offender pay a fitting punishment. Retributive justice: the death penalty.

However, although God is King of the universe, God is not a solitary monarch sitting on a throne. God is a trinity of love relationships between Father, Son, and Spirit. It is clear that God's intention in creating us is to have us participate in this divine fellowship. God is love, and union with Him is His desire for us. But He is also holy—pure goodness and truth. And we have become incorrigibly unholy. We have devolved into self-focused caricatures of what God intended when He created us. As such, we cannot participate in holy fellowship with the triune God unless something changes in us.

Herein lies the dilemma: How can a holy God have intimate relationships with unholy, selfish, fear-ridden creatures who are so far removed from how He originally created them?

God will have His way. He doesn't want anyone to perish, but for everyone to turn to Him because He has a "rehabilitation" plan (*2 Peter* 3:9). He will restore human nature to its original design. He will return His full image and likeness to humanity. He will do whatever it takes, even if it means starting all over again . . . *re*creation.

Jesus said, "Therefore you shall be perfect, just as your Father in heaven is perfect" (*Matthew* 5:48). How can this be? God's intention is to have us live within the fellowship of the Trinity, but He is holy love, and to live within His holy fellowship, we must somehow be transformed. But how can we be transformed back into becoming God's true image bearers? How can this be when we are so incurably addicted to a false self? Is there a plan?

Yes, there is. A divine conspiracy of love called The Incarnation.

Resolving the dilemma

To *redeem* means to recover ownership of something by buying it back. To liberate by paying a ransom. The clearest Biblical context for understanding redemption is the story of Hosea and Gomer, in which Hosea pays to retrieve his repeatedly unfaithful wife off the slave block. Analogously, in God's larger story, Hosea is God, Gomer is Israel, and by extension all humankind. Similar themes in *Isaiah* and the *Book of Revelation* set God's relationship with humans in a husband/wife context. In these analogies, we have depictions of God's passionate love for us, and our unfaithfulness and alienation from Him. Again the question: How can an unholy people be reconciled with a holy God?

"Somebody has to pay," some theologians say, casting the ransom price of redemption as a penalty to be paid in order to fulfill the imperative of justice. But the Biblical context of ransom is not about punishment and penalties, it's about the price needed to rescue, reclaim, and restore our intended identities. We belong to God in the belonging-sense of husband and wife. What is the price God paid to recover and restore this original state of belonging? As we shall see, Jesus laid down His life with 33 years of time, commitment, and the endurance of continual harassment and opposition. Finally, He suffered an excruciatingly cruel death.

On one side of the process of redemption, Jesus Christ is the eternal Son of God, the Father's beloved, who has always loved the Father with all His heart and shared all things with Him in fellowship with Holy Spirit. When the Son of God entered human existence, He did not leave Father and Spirit behind. The Incarnation means that the Triune fellowship set up shop inside human existence here on earth.

On the other side, there is the astonishing truth that the Son of God became *flesh* (*John* 1:14), a word which means human existence from a human mother who had all the inherited traits from her human ancestors, back to Adam. The Word of God, by the power of the Holy Spirit impregnating a human woman, entered into the quagmire of human alienation. As God-man He entered into the fear-laden, lie-infested condition of the human race.

Part of the divine dilemma is that humanity was stuck in a death spiral, a death march. Reorienting the disoriented, twisted condition of mankind was a God-sized problem. Looking at the revolutionary nature of God's incarnational intervention in human history in the person of Jesus Christ, it wouldn't be much of a stretch to attribute these words imaginatively and playfully to God: "This is a huge problem, I will have to take care of it Myself."

The Christian creed has always confessed that Jesus Christ has two distinct natures, divine and human. He is fully God and fully human. He had a divine Father and a human mother. The Incarnation means that although He was the faithful, beloved Son in His relationship with His Father, by having a human mother He put on Adam's glasses and saw through the lens that had marred the Father's face with projections of fear, guilt, and shame. I believe Jesus entered deeply enough into Adamic existence to see and sense this twisted view of God, but He always said "no" to believing any of it.

Jesus the Redeemer entered this lie-infested condition to rescue, reclaim, and take back everything that had been lost and captured by the evil one. How else could God realign the human soul except He Himself enter the depths of the damage and despair, to correct what had been so disfigured and incorrigibly corrupted? This radical realignment meant recovery, restoration, restitution, replacement, up to and including recreation. Let's watch the plan unfold.

Chapter 11

The Death of Sin and the Sin-prone Old Self

In the incarnated Son of God, we find a great paradox: the Word made flesh entered fallen human existence without ceasing to be the faithful Son of the Father, in loving fellowship with the Holy Spirit. How could the One who knows and trusts and loves His Father with His whole being inhabit the blindness, the fearful doubts and outright lies about God embedded in fallen human existence? Something would have to change: Either a fundamental restructuring of God's triune life of love and goodness, or a conversion and fundamental restructuring of human life.

God doesn't change, so the restructuring would have to happen on the human side. Jesus stepped into human existence, refusing to be fallen in it. He stood in Adam's shoes, in Israel's shoes, in our shoes, and He refused to fall into the perverseness of what human nature had devolved into, that is, the mindset and lifestyle of living for oneself, doing whatever it took to survive, to make it on one's own.

The Great Exchange begins

> For we do not have a high priest who is unable to sympathize with our weaknesses, but one who in every respect has been tempted as we are, yet without sin (*Hebrews* 4:15 ESV).

This verse is one of the most powerful and profound verses in the Bible, stating that Jesus, having become flesh by taking on a full human nature, was tempted in every way we have been tempted. However, He never gave in to the fallen human inclination to self-grasping; He always remained in self-giving, in truth, in goodness, in love. It's amazing to imagine the ramifications of this single verse. Step by step, year after year, He loved His Father with all His heart. He refused to believe Adamic lies about His Father. He never gave in to doubts about His Father having His best interests in mind.

Satan's temptations of Jesus (*Matthew* 4; *Luke* 4) tried to prey on the human inclination to trust self rather than to trust God. But in the temptations during His 40-day fast, in the temptations at Gethsemane, and at the cross (to exert His power to save Himself), Jesus always said, "No." Decision by decision, Jesus said "no" to lies, selfishness, disloyalty . . . and "yes" to truth, self-giving, and faithful trust in His Father.

Slowly but surely, Jesus was bending back the distortions of the human soul, back to the nature God had created in humankind. Day by day, Jesus was forging within Himself a tested and true human nature.

Ransom. "Just as the Son of Man did not come to be served but to serve, and to give His life a ransom for many" (*Matthew* 20:28). Our usual way of depicting the process of ransoming someone or delivering them out of captivity involves someone doing something for another person. This might be physically removing or ransoming them from an enemy encampment, or freeing prisoners of war. The story of Hosea and Gomer is literally buying her off a slave block. So, how did Jesus give His life as a ransom for many?

During His years on earth, moment by moment, within His own body and soul, He re-aligned human nature by saying "no" to every counterfeit "human" manifestation that tried to penetrate His soul. He resisted every temptation to *look out for Himself first*—the hallmark of the Adamic self that has developed and alienated every person from God since the Fall.

This "looking after yourself first" is the characteristic that describes us all when we are *tested and fail* to overcome our embedded selfishness. Only Jesus was *tested and succeeded* in overcoming the inward inclination of self-interest over interest in others. He always resisted self-grasping, He always affirmed self-giving. And all of these many choices were steps in freeing the human soul from its captivity—not unlike Hosea giving of his resources to free Gomer from her enslavement.

Here then is a first glimpse of *The Jesus Exchange*. Within Jesus' thinking, feeling, and actions, a continuous exchange was taking place. He rejected prejudice by engaging with Samaritans and Gentiles. In an extremely patriarchal culture, Jesus treated women with dignity and respect. He eschewed religious taboos as He fellowshipped with tax collectors and prostitutes. He exposed the fear and pride that fuel religious legalism, replacing them by lovingly healing people whenever the need arose, even on the sabbath.

The "Divine Exchange" of *2 Corinthians* 5:21 was underway in Him and would continue unabated until the violent and enlivening climax of His death and resurrection. His death would be a final "NO!" to the entire corrupt system of the behaviors of sin, *and* to the selfish cesspool from which oozed the wickedness heaped upon Him—the fallen human heart. And His resurrection would be a new "YES!" to righteousness, truth, and self-giving . . . radiating out from the tomb in all directions from the *tested and true heart* of this God-Man. His risen life is the resource that ransoms us, revives us, and restores us as we choose to live in Him.

Paying the price. "For you were bought with a price" (*1 Corinthians* 6:20). Jesus paid the price; He laid down His life. In the person of Jesus, God expended (paid, laid down) all that He had. He gave His heart, His energy, His time, His endurance . . . to the uttermost extreme of tasting the bitter consequence of sin: death itself.

I'll say it again for emphasis and clarity: In every step of being human on a daily basis, Jesus said "no" to sin and self-grasping ways of dealing with life. He embraced and said "yes" to living human life as God originally intended. No broken trust, no rebellion, no pulling away from the close communion with Father God. For the first time since the Fall, a human being lived a totally righteous life (in thought, moral character, and action). For 33 years He lived in uncensored truth, exposing all forms of evil. In Jesus Christ, a man emerged from the human domain which had been held captive for centuries by the evil one. Finally, a human who was absolutely victorious over evil had set foot on earth.

However, by living so righteously, there was a steep price to pay. Jesus repeatedly challenged the Jewish rulers' corruption of religion for self-gain. He exposed deception, hypocrisy, and superficiality. The Pharisees and Jewish leaders feared and hated Him. They were jealous of His charisma and His many followers. They mocked Him and lied about Him. They made death threats to intimidate Him. Their rage finally boiled over and they enlisted the help of their Roman overseers to execute Him for blasphemy, after He claimed to be the Son of God (*Matthew* 26:63-65).

The Roman Empire was a graphic embodiment of a corrupt world. The Roman rulers fully embraced the old self's commitment to survive by any means necessary, without concern for anyone else. They were only too willing to collude with the wily, wicked Pharisees in helping to do away with someone who might be a threat to their dominance.

So they executed Jesus, adding heinous torture into the process, as a statement the Romans wanted to make to discourage even the thought of rebellion in the masses. He was whipped within an inch of His life, had thorns pounded into His head, was beaten and ridiculed, and finally was executed by the torturous pain of dying by asphyxiation on a cross.

Behind it all, of course, was the arch-narcissist Satan, amplifying human jealousy and hatred with his own dark spiritual power. There at the cross, we find this dark fountainhead of pride and lawlessness pouring out his hate-fueled anger, intent on destroying God's creation and anyone aligned with God. Jesus was a major threat to his reign. One act of self-grasping would do it—abort His sacrificial mission by exerting energy to save Himself from torture and death. But Jesus did not succumb. He endured. He drank the full cup of poison to the last bitter dregs.

Who tortured and killed Jesus?

There is a 2018 film, *God Bless the Broken Road*, in which the widow of an Army sergeant, killed on patrol in Afghanistan, struggles with anger towards God. She and her nine-year-old daughter miss him terribly, and their lives are in emotional disarray. She doesn't receive answers for why God would allow this to happen, and her faith falters. There is a soldier in her church who was in her husband's squad, still recovering from a serious wound inflicted on him during the same ambush that killed her husband. Towards the end of the film, the woman and the soldier have a conversation, and she comes to know what happened on that day.

The squad was on patrol to discover and disarm IED's (improvised explosive devices). Driving through a narrow pass, they were suddenly ambushed by Afghani Mujahideen. The wounded soldier narrating the events to the widow, as they sat in a church pew, told how he was wounded by a sniper bullet and left out in the open, unable to move to safety. His sergeant, the woman's husband, ran to him and dragged him to safety behind an armored vehicle. However, while dragging him to safety, the sergeant was hit by another sniper's bullet. It was a mortal wound, and he died on the ground, lying next to the wounded man. The soldier then explained to the widow that the squad eventually overcame the Afghani rebels and safely returned to base.

The story ends as the recovering soldier turns to the widow and plaintively tells her that her husband did not die in vain. His own life was saved, and he realized God's hand was in his rescue. He turned to the Lord, became a believer, and now has eternal life as well. The woman dissolves into a heap of tears, her doubts and struggles resolved, and she recovers a vibrant faith in God.

While watching the film, I had a Eureka! moment. When Sergeant Darren was shot and killed, I was struck with a wide-eyed analogy: The bullet that was fired at Jesus on the cross was not God firing a bullet (penalty, punishment, wrath), with Jesus stepping in like a Secret Service agent taking the bullet meant for us. No, the bullet was sin, selfishness, and the evil one.[6] These are the forces, like the sniper's bullet, actively engaged in capturing us, harassing us, trying to snuff us out.

Jesus told us (*John* 10:10) that it was Satan's mission to steal, kill, and destroy. It was the wrath of the old self (obsessed with having its own way, like its master, Satan) that poured itself out onto Jesus. Jesus took the attacks of opposition and threats during His whole lifetime

---

[6] God's holy wrath is unquestionably stored up to be delivered like a consuming fire against all evil, which will include those who have chosen the ways of evil, wickedness, and iniquity. This will take place in the future, on the Day of the Lord, the Day of Judgment (*Matthew 11:24; 2 Peter 3:10; John 12:48*).

as He stood in truth, humility, and love. Finally, the "sniper's bullet" ambush set for Jesus was orchestrated by the Pharisees and religious leaders, and carried out by the Romans. All were pawns of Satan.

I believe the demonic plan was to thwart Jesus' mission of giving mankind eternal life. Jesus' mission was designed to defeat Satan, to destroy his intent to keep us in captivity to sin and death. God's plan was a kind of "conspiracy of love," in which He allowed all this evil to play itself out on Jesus so that God could unfold the drama of love triumphing over hatred and evil. As Jesus said, He voluntarily laid down His life, He didn't have it taken from Him (*John* 10:17).

I was once a soldier in Satan's army, under his command, living within the kingdom of self, in open rebellion to the Kingdom of God. My lifestyle and character were mostly a display of the egocentric poison poured out on Jesus. My own disease and rebellion were part of the forces that tried to snuff out the Son of Man. I believe that there are only two kingdoms: the kingdom of darkness and the Kingdom of God. By God's merciful lovingkindness, His forgiving and transforming love, together with my choice to say "yes" to Him in response, I am a converted terrorist. Thank you, Jesus.

There is a poignant foreshadowing of Calvary in Isaiah's prophecy about the Suffering Servant: "All of us have wandered about like sheep; we each have turned to his own way; and Yahweh let fall on Him the iniquity of us all" (*Isaiah* 53:6 LEB). Iniquity is sheer wickedness, the cumulative reality of all sinful acts and the sin-saturated hearts from which all human evil has flowed. And *1 Peter* 2:24 ESV tells us that "He himself bore our sins in his body on the tree, that we might die to sin and live to righteousness."

I am convinced that Jesus bore our sin and our self-centered, counterfeit human nature in His body on the cross by having the entire rotten mess inflicted upon Him. Selfishness, fear, jealousy, hatred, revenge, betrayal, lying, torture—the ugly face of our first-Adam way of life. "Doing it my way." And it all ends in evil, violence, and death. The wages of sin are indeed death.

Also, Jesus took upon Himself all of the human wounds inflicted upon one another from living for centuries apart from God: shame, anxiety, rejection, fear, and all sorts of sorrows. "He is despised and rejected by men, a Man of sorrows and acquainted with grief . . . . Surely He has borne our griefs and carried our sorrows . . . ." (*Isaiah* 53:3-4).

He took it all, sin and wounds.

The whole conspiracy of love devised by the triune fellowship of God has always been to find the way for humankind to get off the path that leads to the devastation caused by living apart from communion with God. This is a path that eventually winds its way into eternal separation from God (sometimes called the "second death," See *Revelation* 20:6). In the Bible, the heart of God yearns for our restoration and reunion. It isn't a matter of what we deserve, it's a matter of discerning what God intends. He wants us back with Him.

However, real restoration includes radical exchange, and this can sometimes be a difficult reality to face. I too wince when I fully face the fact that my road-rage, for example, is a manifestation of something in my heart that was also active in the hearts of the angry men who delivered the whipping to Jesus' ravaged back. My anger and egocentricity are somewhere on that same old-self spectrum that was manifested at Calvary, including pounding in the thorns and nails. I cringe sometimes when I realize that mindsets and heartsets I myself have harbored were present within the energy exerted to drive in those thorns and nails.

I am painfully sobered when I realize in my heart that the answer to the song's verse, "Were you there when they crucified my Lord?" is "Yes, I was there, and not just as a spectator. I was a participant by my selfishness and by my wounds." Jesus took them all, sin and wounds. Fortunately, the Holy Spirit has not left me to wallow in that truth alone. There is astonishingly more, as depicted in this beautiful paraphrase of *Romans* 8:1-4 The Remedy Bible:

> Therefore, those who trust in Christ Jesus are no longer destined to die, because through Christ Jesus the law of love has cleansed and healed them from the law of selfishness and death. The written law was powerless to restore trust, as it could merely diagnose the infection of distrust and selfishness pervading us all. God accomplished this resto-

ration of the character of love in humans by sending his own Son in human flesh to eradicate selfishness from humanity, reveal the truth about God, expose the lies of Satan, and reveal what happens when the infection of sin is not cured. And so he condemned the infection of selfishness as the destroying element in sinful humanity in order that the law of love—the principle upon which life is based—might be fully restored in us, who no longer live according to selfish desires, but in harmony with the Spirit of love and truth.

Chapter 12

A Whole Lot of Pouring Going On

Many times I have heard and read the phrase, "God poured out His wrath on Jesus," as supposedly descriptive of what happened in those moments when Jesus died on the cross. That phrase is not in the Bible. I believe lots of "pouring" was going on, but not God pouring out punishment and penalty on Jesus' body and soul.

1. Arch-narcissist Satan poured out his anger and hatred against God's Kingdom of Love, using principalities and powers that worked through the cultural systems of Jewish religion and Roman authority. The enemy poured out his hatred through jealousy, lies, and the violent death of Jesus, in an attempt to thwart Him from accomplishing His mission of redemption. Satan orchestrated and poured out the full arsenal of false-self weapons upon Jesus. He was ". . . tempted in every way, just as we are—yet he did not sin" (*Hebrews* 4:15 NIV). Just one act of *self-first* would foil the rescue operation, like succumbing to the taunt, "Let Him now come down from the cross . . ." (*Matthew* 27:42).

2. Jesus poured out His final bending of human nature back into God's original design of self-giving by sacrificially absorbing and enduring every blow of the enemy. He did not retaliate in any way. Here was the innocent, pure Lamb of God suffering and enduring the worst miscarriage of "justice" this world has ever known. He swallowed and absorbed the whole rotten thing, and in doing so He turned the tables and, wrestler-like, flipped and pinned the Prince of Darkness. Death had no claim on Jesus because He remained sinless throughout His life, sinless to the very end. Self-giv-

ing overcame self-grasping; love overcame hate; light overwhelmed darkness.

Here was the extension of "God is love" into the human domain, as finally a human being lived out the fullness of what it means to be the image of God. It was a God-sized job, one only God could do. And He did it, for our eternal wellbeing and for us to have abundant life (*John* 10:10) rather than to continue on our lost, separated-from-God death march. Jesus said, simply and conclusively, "It is finished." He had cleared the way to set us on a new path, a new way—Himself.

Throughout His years on earth, in all of His temptations, Jesus refused to put Himself first, and He was faithful to the end. *Self-first* had to die. *Self-first* was the target, and it died when Jesus chose *others-first*. He paid the full price, that is, He paid what it took to defeat sin and self-first. What it took was God Himself coming to inhabit the human soul, killing self-deification through self-giving love. He expunged embedded soul cancer, moment by moment, until the final "no" to putting Himself first.

> *He did what it took: He laid down His life, from birth to death. He paid the price of expending Himself fully. He poured out His whole life. He went all in.*

3. God's judgment poured out on this monstrous old self which manifested itself so viciously and violently upon Jesus. *Romans* 6:6 clearly reveals: "We know that our old self was crucified with Him in order that the body of sin might be brought to nothing, so that we would no longer be enslaved to sin." On Good Friday, there were earthquakes and darkened, stormy skies. Something died. Jesus died, but something was dragged to death through Him. The death that would not rise again was that of sin and of the false self. Jesus took them upon Himself and overpowered them: "In this

way also, the Messiah . . . slaughtered in his Person the sins [the entire body of sin] of the many . . ." (*Hebrews* 9:28 Aramaic Bible).

Human nature was cleansed and purged. A disease had been expunged. Something was surgically removed. On that day, the veil of the temple in Jerusalem was torn from top to bottom in those very moments that the old self was judged and crucified. In this way, Jesus was our substitute because the surgical correction of our inner bend towards self was something we could not do ourselves. However, it needed to be done if ever our souls were to be truly reconciled with our holy God.

He did it all . . . for us. The heavy curtain in the Jewish temple separated the place where sinful humans congregated from the place called the Holy of Holies, where the holy, sinless presence of the Lord hovered in the Ark of the Covenant. No one could enter that inner space except the High Priest on special occasions. When the curtain was torn on Good Friday, a sinless human, tried and true, was now living on the earth, one who could dwell in the presence of God. He could approach God's throne because He was sinless, not only in His outward behavior but He was also pure and blameless in His heart.

Jesus made this tearing of the veil possible so we could now abide in Him and thus be reconciled with God and be restored to union with Him: "Let us therefore come boldly to the throne of grace, that we may obtain mercy and find grace to help in time of need" (*Hebrews* 4:16). On Good Friday, the process of reconciliation had begun, and we are invited to dive into Jesus and share in the fruit of His loving labor as He replicates His nature in us. "Come boldly" the Word declares.

I believe that God's attention has always been focused in on the disease of sin, the selfish corruption of the human heart. God hates wickedness (*Hebrews* 1:9) and dealt it the death-blow in Christ Jesus. I think of Good Friday as the beginning of the Day of the Lord, that Day in the future when the final death of eternal separation from God will take place. Good Friday was a day of judgment for the old Adamic nature, the end of the heritage of Adam from the first creation. A new Adam and a new lineage were soon to be born.

There had never been a more "perfect storm" of intense hatred directed at a Being who is the embodiment of love. Never was there a more perfectly innocent person executed in such a cosmic miscarriage of justice. But God turned it into the greatest restoration of His justice: setting things aright, according to His design, and according to His nature. In Christ Jesus, the foundational force of Love that runs the universe was re-infused into humankind.

4. Jesus let His blood be poured out, His final "no" to sin and selfishness. He didn't retaliate. He didn't call down legions of angels to save Himself. This pouring out was also His final "yes" to self-giving love. His blood called out "Mercy," not "retribution." Here was the fulfillment of the blood-sprinkling upon the Mercy Seat on this new and final Day of Atonement, when Jesus said, "Forgive them," and all sin was washed away not just covered or provisionally cleansed. God poured out His forgiveness for all sins, for all time. He canceled all penalties, debt, and shame. Sin was removed from human nature by forgiveness, just as the sin-prone old self was expunged by love triumphing over hate.

To clarify this last comment, the next chapter will focus entirely on how the forgiveness facet of the Incarnation jewel is intertwined with the transformation facet.

Chapter 13

A Tale of Two Facets

A few years ago, I was attending a worship service in which congregants were speaking out prayers of thanksgiving for what Jesus had done for them. One prayer offered was, "Thank you Jesus for taking the wounds I deserved but you took them instead."

In the previous two chapters, I presented the Scriptural evidence that Jesus had taken our actual sin and suffering upon Himself, not that He had taken on a God-sent punishment as a substitute sufferer of our penalty. Is it true that every person *deserves* to be tortured and killed as the penalty for sin? Does your mother deserve to have sharp thorns driven deep into her head by the flat side of a sword? Does your 15-year-old son deserve to be stripped naked, whipped within an inch of his life, and then be tortured by hanging on a cross until he dies by asphyxiation? Such is the corner the penal substitution theorists have painted themselves into by their punitive version of substitutionary atonement.

Roman crucifixion was a form of execution that manifested the demonic character of cruelty; it had not a smidgen of lovingkindness in it, from its gruesome beginning to its grisly end. In looking at the sufferings of Jesus, what was really on display was an extreme expression of *the false self*: putting others down to raise oneself up, brutish control, retaliation. Plus, all the suffering that this false self inflicts on humankind.

So, what are we to think about these wounds of Jesus if we look at them through a restorative rather than a punitive lens? For starters, in the Incarnation, God entered our wretchedness and brokenness through Jesus Christ. He came into a world that was filled with abuse, oppression, and injustice. By standing in right alignment with His Father, Jesus placed Himself in *solidarity* with the poor and oppressed around Him. He made Himself vulnerable to the same abuse and injustice that Rome and Jewish leaders heaped upon the populace.

As foreshadowed in *Isaiah* 53:4, "... Surely He has borne our griefs and carried our sorrows." By participating in our wretched condition, He took upon Himself all the shame, humiliation, abuse, and betrayal that this world has known, or will know.

He also absorbed the abusive sin of the wicked Pharisees, the cruelty of the Roman soldiers, and the systemic evil of old-life ways woven into the institutions of religious, economic, and political power. "... And the Lord has laid on Him the iniquity of us all" (*Isaiah* 53: 6).

The divine plan was to allow all of it, wounds and sin alike, to be heaped upon Jesus, until He was a saturated sponge. And in that state of saturation, the switch was flipped. Love stepped in and overpowered wickedness, like an almost-pinned wrestler flipping and pinning his opponent. Love overcame the whole system of violence and retributive justice. Nonviolent enemy-love overpowered ego-inflated hate. Self-giving drove out all selfishness. So, a significant part of the divine plan was a transfusion-like emptying out of the diseased human heart (old life).

Another layer, or facet, was forgiveness. On the cross, Jesus practiced what He had preached in His Sermon on the Mount: "You have heard that it was said, 'an eye for an eye and a tooth for a tooth.' But I tell you not to resist an evil person.... You have heard that it was said, 'You shall love your neighbor and hate your enemy.' But I say to you, love your enemies, bless those who curse you, do good to those who hate you, and pray for those who spitefully use you and persecute you" (*Matthew* 5:38-44).

The torture and the cross demonstrated in graphic action the "eye for an eye" system of retributive justice in full swing: "This is what you get for your rejection of our religious system," sneered the Jewish leaders. "This is what you get for threatening our dominance," said the Romans. "Crucify Him, crucify Him," cried out the cowardly mob, fearful that retribution might be heaped on *them* unless they went along with the execution.

This is where the entire system of the corrupted nature of humankind had led in its blind egocentricity—the murder of the Son of Man, the totally innocent Lamb of God. God's response? He forgave them/us all. The Lamb of God took away the sins of the world by sacrificially letting the whole rotten mess be inflicted upon Himself, to the point of death, and His love response washed it all away by the power of *forgiveness*.

The Cross is not about penalty payment, it is about mercy. Good Friday is not about divine wrath, it is about divine love—the love even of enemies, as preached by Jesus in *Matthew* 5. On the cross, Jesus demonstrated that "love your enemies" includes forgiving them! Here is a powerful foundation stone of the New Covenant. Calvary is not a place where we see a violent God pouring out His wrath on Jesus as a punishment substitute. Calvary is where we see how violent our fallen civilization is, and God's response of forgiveness. [7]

If we fix our eyes on Jesus there on the cross, we can see that what He endured and absorbed on the cross were both our sins and our wounds. It's our stuff we see there. If we are able to see and accept that reality, then we can receive God's forgiveness, as well as receive the healing He offers through the other powerful component of the New Covenant: transformation by exchange transfusion. Forgiving love, restorative love, healing love. This love offers humanity a way out of the vicious cycles of sin and woundedness in which we all have become hopelessly entangled.

Foreshadows and fulfillment

When examining the words *sacrifice* and *atonement*, we need to keep our eyes fixed on Jesus and on the New Testament writers—especially when referring to bloodshed and atonement as part of forgiveness. In Chapter 7, I presented the analogy of seeing the Old Testament as a kind of moonlight reflecting the Light of the world, Jesus Himself. Everything in the Old Testament points to Jesus.

Blood sacrifices. In the early history of Israel, the Law of Mo-

---

[7] Although, as was mentioned in previous chapters and will be further developed in Chapter 14, the wrath of God was indeed poured out in judgment on the systemic sin that had insinuated itself into all human souls, except the soul of Jesus. That systemic corruption of the heart (old self, false self), so viciously inflicted upon Jesus, was crucified in Christ Jesus, and in Him condemned forever. See *Romans* 6:6.

ses required blood sacrifices for the cleansing of sin. But prophets later challenged this requirement: "I do not delight in the blood of bulls, or of lambs or goats" (*Isaiah* 1:11). King David said: "Sacrifice and offering You do not desire .... Burnt offering and sin offering You have not required" (*Psalms* 40:6). Hosea tells us that God desires "steadfast love and not sacrifice" (*Hosea* 6:6).

In the New Testament, the verses related to blood sacrifices are often taken out of context, thereby making the Old Testament "moonlight" into a bright-light "truth." An example is in the *Epistle to the Hebrews* where we find the following statement: "Indeed, under the Law almost everything is purified with blood, and without the shedding of blood there is no forgiveness of sins" (*Hebrews* 9:22 NRSV). But the writer goes on to say, in Chapter 10:5-9:

> Consequently, when Christ came into the world, He said, "Sacrifices and offerings you have not desired, but a body you have prepared for me; in burnt offerings and sin offerings you have taken no pleasure. Then I said, 'See, God, I have come to do your will, O God' (in the scroll of the book it is written of me)". When he said above, "You have neither desired nor taken pleasure in sacrifice and offerings and sin offerings" (these are offered according to the law), then he added, "See, I have come to do your will." He abolishes the first in order to establish the second.

In other words, the New Testament writer of *Hebrews* understood that God had abolished ritual animal sacrifice in order to establish a wholly new solution in Christ Jesus: "See, I have come to do your will." The old system was ended. The new was a demonstration of God's will. Jesus faithfully obeyed His Father by demonstrating divine forgiveness, even while being crucified! Jesus told the sacrifice-obsessed Pharisees: "Go and learn what this means, 'I desire mercy, not sacrifice'" (*Matthew* 9:13).

Whereas Old Testament sacrifice was a legal requirement under the Law, the New Testament sacrifice of Jesus was doing something no animal blood sacrifice could do: be an outpouring of self-giving love, forgiveness, and mercy. The sprinkling of a heifer's or lamb's blood on the Mercy Seat in the temple on Yom Kippur was a provisional cleansing of what was to come when Messiah arrived on the scene and poured out God's forgiveness in a sacrifice that was fully effective in complete cleansing of sin *and* sin-prone corrupted human nature.

Once the Messiah came, the radical reality of full forgiveness and mercy that He enacted on the cross was, and is, a sun-brightness truth that should pull our gaze fully upon Jesus. What we see in Him is a revelation of the true nature of our God, who is Lovingkindness, slow to anger, and full of compassion and mercy (*Psalms* 145:8 AMP).

In gazing upon Jesus, we see this inner core of God on full display, for all to see. In Him, the meaning of sacrifice has changed from a ritual requirement to an act of love that brings forgiveness and healing. In Him we come to the end of blood sacrifices. In Jesus, "sacrifice" and "blood poured out" = self-giving and love poured out. The operative words are *self-giving love*, not blood sacrifice. There we were, enemies of God, crucifying Him, and He forgave us. Mercy poured out. Who could have known that there were such far reaches of the words: "God is love"?

Jesus reveals that the far reaches of love include loving our enemies, forgiveness, and mercy. The cross wasn't something God did, the cross is who God is! God didn't need the cross in order to forgive; the cross was God's chosen way to *demonstrate* and *manifest* His forgiving heart. As well, the cross was God's chosen way to expunge (crucify) the selfishness-infested old life.

Jesus said to Philip, "When you see Me, you see the Father" (*John* 14:9). So, as we look at Jesus on the cross, I believe we are seeing the mercy and compassion that are intrinsic aspects of God's character. The sin of the whole world was allowed to be inflicted upon Jesus, and this innocent, blameless Lamb, in obediently doing whatever He saw His Father doing (*John* 5:19) says, "Father, forgive them for they do not know what they do" (*Luke* 23:34).

Atonement. In the Old Testament, atonement has several connotations. Two of the main ones are *cleansing* and *covering*. On the Day of Atonement (Yom Kippur), the blood of the sacrificial animal would be sprinkled on the Mercy Seat in the Holy of Holies, as a sin offering. It was a ritualistic expression of cleansing humans of sins that had accumulated during the previous year. Further, on that same Day of Atonement, a goat was sent into the desert carrying those accumulated sins of the people. The scapegoat ritual was also a kind of cleansing or purging.

In a second meaning, the Hebrew word for atonement, *Kippur*, means *covering*. The word was first used in the Bible in *Genesis* 6:14, in the instructions given to Noah to apply tar-like pitch on the inside and outside of the ark to keep water from seeping in. The pitch *covered* the boat. Many of the animal sacrifices of the Old Testament put a person's sins out of God's sight by covering them, by *atoning* for them. So, "the blood that makes atonement for the soul" (*Leviticus* 17:11) means that "the blood makes a cover for the soul."

Whether cleansing or covering, the rituals were temporary, provisional measures. Permanent removal would be the final solution—a solution that was not expected to occur until Messiah arrived (*Hebrews* 10:1). Well, Messiah arrived and we are permanently cleansed when we dive into Jesus and let Him wash our sins away. His blood does not *cover*, His sacrificial, forgiving love *fully cleanses*. The New Testament is full of this new arrangement: "And you know that He was manifested to take away our sins" (*1 John* 3:5). See also *1 Peter* 2:24 and *Hebrews* 9:28.

Forgiveness and Restoration: facets shining forth God's heart of Love and Holiness

Forgiveness. So, Yom Kippur, the Day of Atonement, is a shadow that is absorbed by the sunlight: In Christ Jesus, my sins are forgiven, taken away, removed. The dirtiness of all my sinful behaviors (past, present, future) is washed away. Whatever there might be of any penalty, debt, shame, curse—all of it is mercifully pardoned, forgiven, erased, washed away.

My soul has been cleansed and will always be cleaned up whenever I turn to You, Lord. Your forgiveness is always there, waiting for me to receive. That is too wondrous for me to fully grasp. As I abide in You here, I ask to tap into Your capacity to receive fully what You have so freely given. I receive what You have done, and who You are, and who You have revealed our Father to be: Merciful Lovingkindness. Thank you, Jesus. Thank you, Father.[8]

The Bible states that "God is love." Jesus demonstrates and reveals that forgiveness is an intrinsic part of this love. Before Calvary, Jesus had already forgiven the sins of the adulterous woman (*John* 8:10-11); the woman who washed Jesus' feet (*Luke* 7:48); and the paralytic (*Matthew* 9:3). Convincingly, in *Matthew*, Chapter 18, Jesus tells of a master who forgave a servant of millions of dollars. He was released from his debt and there was no longer any need for payment to be made.

Similar to the master in *Matthew* 18, out of the abundance of His heart God forgives us. And God requires us to activate in all of our relationships this same attribute of Himself, without any conditions or thoughts about payment. We are to express the same compassion and mercy that God pours out upon His whole creation, not because of any payment, but because this forgiveness is already in His heart, and we are made to be like Him. The sacrifice of Jesus is this self-giving love poured out.

Restoration. Yes, Jesus paid an immense price to redeem us, to deal with unholy selfishness that had ravaged human hearts. He laid down His life every day in forging real human nature, one that replaced self-grasping with self-giving. This was a painful and costly process.

The ransom price He paid was what it cost God to restore and reclaim what had been so disfigured. Imagine the *Mona Lisa* painting ruined by smearing lurid lipstick and greasepaint into the countenance of the painting. It would be a time-consuming, energy-consuming, costly project to restore that work of art to its original state of beauty. And it would be a restoration that the artist, Leonardo da Vinci, would want to undertake himself.

Such was the project God accomplished in Christ Jesus. There

---

[8] While writing this section, Holy Spirit touched my heart, prompting me to experience that I had not yet fully accepted God's full forgiveness (perhaps a residual vestige of the lie I had believed for years: that I had "gone over the limit" of sinning during my years of rebellion). So, what reads like a prayer in this paragraph *is* a prayer! I share it for anyone who may need their hearts touched similarly.

is a Scriptural verse that highlights this artistic reference: "For we are God's own handiwork, His workmanship, recreated in Christ Jesus, born anew" (*Ephesians* 2:10 AMP). The Greek word Paul chose for "workmanship" was *poiema*, from which the word poem is derived. Poiema is used to convey a sense of God the Master Craftsman restoring His works of art to their original state as reflections of Himself. We are His masterpieces.

To be sure, whoever ruined such a painting would have a large penalty debt to pay for such felonious behavior, and God has no doubt been greatly offended by what we have done, and continue to do, to the beautiful human nature He has given us. But there is a difference between the *debt* of sin and the *restitution* needed to restore what has been disfigured.

I believe that Jesus canceled the penalty debt of sin (*Colossians* 2:14) through God's merciful heart of forgiveness. When anyone turns from a life of self-centeredness and comes to God like the prodigal son, he or she may receive this forgiveness. The steep price Jesus paid was to restore what had been disfigured, to make holy what had been besmirched with unholy selfishness. By so doing, He gave everyone a second chance at being our true self, the "Mona Lisa" God intends for each of us to become. God does this restitution through and in Christ Jesus, as we come to Him, abide in Him, eat and drink Him.

So, one facet of the redemption diamond is *forgiveness* and the other is *transformation/restitution/restoration*. Both are dazzling displays of our Creator.

We speak of a "Finished Work" taking place at the cross. Yet, it was not a completely finished work. At the cross, God's forgiveness removed all penalty, guilt, and shame. And Jesus expunged the old self from human nature. But nature abhors a vacuum. The other half of Jesus' mission was yet to take place: an infilling, a breathing in of life . . . a new creation.

Chapter 14

Arise, My Son!

While writing *Becoming the Likeness of Jesus*, I had a vision which I will share because it depicts the restorative justice dimension of the Incarnation that I have discovered and am endeavoring to express.

I saw a large tree in a garden. A prominent branch had broken off and was lying on the ground. The branch's leaves had wilted, and parasitical weeds had sprung up, wrapping themselves tightly around all the offshoots growing out from the branch. Life was slowly being drained out of the branch by these weeds. The branch had been on the ground for a long time and rot had eaten holes through the bark, penetrating well into the interior. Various insects and other creatures feasted on the rotting parts. The weakened branch tried valiantly to survive but, however gradual, death was inevitable.

Then the large tree from which the branch had broken off began bending its entire formidable crown and trunk down towards the detached branch in a gesture of embrace. Without detaching from the tree, a significant segment of the bending tree (branch-like but also trunk-like) reached down and enfolded the branch on the ground, gently and tenderly lifting it up and taking it to its breast. This trunk/branch partially morphed into a figure that I knew was Jesus. As the branch enfolded the detached branch into Himself, He completely absorbed all the rottenness, bugs, and weeds, replacing them with His healthy, robust life.

In the final scene of the vision, Jesus fully embraced the detached branch, grafting it into Himself, and it became one with the Tree-Branch (God-Man). The branch was becoming enlivened and restored, and was showing signs of resembling once again its former state of being an organic part of the tree. There was also a glimmer of understanding that, in its new state, the branch would grow into something better than it had ever been—better even than its original state, before it had detached.

As I ponder this vision, it seems significant to point out that there was an absorption and disposal of the corruption that had invaded the detached branch. And there was an immediate, regenerative restoration of the branch upon being lovingly re-attached to the tree. Life-giving sap now flowed into the grafted branch. However, it was clear that gradual yet steady exchanges of new cells replacing old cells would accomplish a complete transformation in the branch (from deadened and weakened to enlivened and strong) until the branch would truly belong to and be fully united with the tree.

As the vision subsided, I had a sense of completion and wholeness, accompanied by feelings of peace and joy. In this vision, God as *love* and as *holy* flowed together in an integrated way.

I believe that adoption and union with God are the heart of the Christian Gospel. Forgiveness is a powerful truth, as described in Chapter 13. However, there is another facet that gleams radiantly from the Incarnation diamond: the facet of transformation. Yes, we have offended God. Yes, we have gone our own way, trying to survive on our own, perverting and twisting our God-given natures into unholy caricatures of our original design. We desperately need God's mercy and forgiveness. But it distorts the truth of the Gospel to separate God's holiness from His love. Forgiveness serves a higher goal of restoring our union with God. True, we need our sins pardoned, but we also need our hearts and minds transformed because God has said, "Be holy, for I am holy" (*1 Peter* 1:16).

When we narrowly focus on forgiveness as a pardon for our *sinful behaviors*, the redemption of our souls is incomplete. We can end up with the idea that Jesus' righteousness was merely imputed to us legally, and we can claim it as our own if we believe in Him. This can easily slip into an image of something akin to putting a silk robe on a pig . . . unless we speak of real transformation of the human heart in the same breath as we speak of forgiveness. A word-study of the Scriptural meanings for *justification* and *righteousness* yields a rich discovery of both words as referring to the presence of experiential goodness in a person.

In our fallen state, we aren't pigs. Underneath it all, each person has been created in God's image and likeness. Redemption has to do with forgiveness, but redemption must also be seen through the lens of God's clear intention to deliver us from the animal-like states we sometimes exhibit when living through our false selves. We need to have our hearts made holy. The Holy Spirit does not *impute* Jesus' righteousness, He *imparts* Jesus' righteous nature into us.

Radical *transformation* needs to be presented alongside *forgiveness* as an intrinsic part of the Gospel, or we have a truncated Gospel. In many denominations, this truth is still hidden from believers. Scripture bears out the reality that Jesus' perfect righteousness enfolds us *while we become* His righteousness (*2 Corinthians* 5:21) . . . until Jesus Christ is formed in us (*Galatians* 4:19). We are not to continue merely wearing Jesus' risen human nature as an external covering; while we abide in Him, we are gradually being transformed into His very likeness.

A clear portrayal of the integration of God as holy love comes into focus by considering Christ's death and resurrection as two halves of a whole, rather than as separate events.

The Gospel as death *and* resurrection

The Scripture verse that has been at the heart of my life and ministry is *2 Corinthians* 5:21, "For He made Him who knew no sin to be sin for us, that we might become the righteousness of God in Him." It is a significant verse for understanding Jesus' death and resurrection as two phases of one event. It is noteworthy that Jesus Himself *always* spoke of going to Jerusalem to die and to rise again. He kept the two together.

In *2 Corinthians* 5:21, we can see two phases of the exchange process. One is the sin/evil/death phase, the other is the righteousness/goodness/life phase. We could say that the first phase is emptying out the old (death), and the second phase is a filling in with the new (life).

Phase One: Death. "For He made Him who knew no sin to be sin for us . . . ." Every 'no' that Jesus said to every temptation was an emptying out of the self-centered inclination embedded in fallen human nature. By saying "no" He was removing self-centered inclinations from human nature, clearing out the Adamic self from humanity. He did this, decision by decision, culminating on the cross in a last, definitive "No!" to the temptation to come down off the cross and save Himself, and the temptation to believe that His Father had abandoned Him.

All the wickedness of humankind was laid on Jesus. He absorbed it all and He resisted it all—the behavior of sin as well as the corrupted human soul from which all wicked behavior originates.

Through the colossal mercy that poured out from God through Jesus on the cross, the worst injustice this world has ever known was forgiven. All our iniquity and wickedness were right there at the cross, being laid on Jesus; and we all have been forgiven, cleansed, purged. The self-giving love of God flowed out through the forgiving, cleansing stream of Jesus' blood as it poured out upon the earth and upon all humankind.

Phase Two: Resurrection. ". . . that we might become the righteousness of God in Him." If Phase One is about emptying, purging, and releasing, Phase Two, the resurrection, is about infilling, replacing, and re-creating. At the resurrection, God replaced the stripped away counterfeit nature with the nature of the "second Adam" (*1 Corinthians* 15:45-49). This risen nature was Jesus' righteousness, goodness, and communion with His Father.

In Phase Two, we peer into the amazing reality of the resurrection of Jesus. For 33 years He had been resisting evil, never succumbing to any temptation. He allowed His human nature to be tested and then filled with all the righteous responses He gave in rebuffing the constant assaults of the evil one. The enemy clamored for Him to give in just once, thereby satisfying the inclination to look out for Himself first. But there was no "fall" in Jesus, no breach of trust with His Father, no break in His communion with Father God. He was tested and proven to be true.

The Holy Spirit, the Ruach Hakodesh, rushed in, surging into every nook and cranny of Jesus' body and soul, joyfully and unreservedly raising Him up from the dead. The tomb became a womb. The Wind of the Holy Spirit gathered together the entirety of Jesus' human nature with all the righteousness and goodness Jesus had forged. He had perfectly lived out what it means to live as God intended for humans when He created them as the *imago Dei*, the very likeness of God. Death had no claim on Him. He was sinless in His behavior, and His heart was also unblemished.

A human being, triumphant over sin and death, now walked the earth. And this Man was also God. He had the power to give His new life away to whomever would come to Him. "Come to Me," He says (*Matthew* 11: 28). My paraphrase: "Come to Me, spiritually consume Me, drink Me, abide in Me, that you might become in yourselves what I accomplished within Myself. I did it all for you, so you can be changed into being like Me. I am your Redeemer, your Life-giver, and I am your Brother, your Friend."

Jesus' death and resurrection accomplished real, experiential reconciliation

The process of reconciliation is to bring back into union what has been separated. Nothing in God needs to change or be appeased, but we need to be cleaned up, healed, and restored. As governed by the selfishness of our old nature, with Satan as its master, we are not fit to be God's companions for eternity. All our sins and our false way of life cause us to be separated from God and unholy before Him. Reconciliation means to remedy this situation, to restore a former state of union and communion, for that is God's intention for us. Let's look at how this was done in Jesus.

Death. Jesus Christ (Son of God and Son of Man) allowed sin, wounds, and the entire false self of humanity to be inflicted upon Himself. He absorbed all that has separated humankind from God, and the Godhead/Trinity judged that old self and condemned it as unworthy of continuing to serve as human nature. On Calvary, the old self was declared to be a counterfeit and was cast out and disposed of (*Romans* 6:6). All of this happened within the Son of Man. In Christ Jesus, humanity was cleaned out by forgiveness and by the surgical removal of our cancerous old self. When grafted into Him, we partake of all that He accomplished.

Resurrection. When Holy Spirit filled the entirety of Jesus' human nature with righteousness and goodness, this same Spirit was planning to fill and replace the hearts and souls of all humankind who would come to Jesus. Everything Jesus did was self-giving love for all of us (*John* 3:16).

The resurrection was a *recreation* moment for the human race. In addition to being called the second Adam, Jesus was also called the "firstborn of many brothers and sisters" (*Romans* 8:29). Many times this verse from *Romans* has come up in this discovery project as a succinct way of expressing that something was done in the crucible of Christ's human nature. Yet, that was only the beginning. All that He did within Himself was done so we might eat Him and drink Him, that is, receive in ourselves what He accomplished in Himself. Abiding in Him, we become His brothers and sisters.

In the death and resurrection of Jesus we have experiential reconciliation, not merely a legal transaction through which we were given the right to claim Jesus' righteousness as our own. The verse in *2 Corinthians* 5:21 says "that we might *become* [italics mine] the righteousness of God in Him." We become what we eat. We are to eat and drink Jesus so we can become like Him.

That includes following Him into dying to old life and being filled with His new life. We are to be the same kind of "sponge" as we allow Holy Spirit to squeeze out the old and refill us with the new. A process of real becoming: ". . . to put off your old self, which belongs to your former manner of life and is corrupt through deceitful desires . . . and to put on the new self, created to be like God in true righteousness and holiness" (*Ephesians* 4:22-24 ESV).

As we abide in Jesus, living as a branch grafted into the Vine, we are indeed grafted back into union with God our Father. Within Jesus, we are made fit to exist in the presence of a pure and holy God, to be able to have fellowship with our Father/Son/Holy Spirit God.

Jesus has rehabilitated and restored the human race back into communion with God. This communion is the real reconciliation Jesus offers when He says, "Dive into Me, the water is fine" [my words]. Read His life-giving words of *John* 7:37-38: "If anyone thirsts, let him come to Me and drink. He who believes in [into] Me, as the Scripture has said, out of his heart will flow rivers of living water."

He has made the way for us to return, to be made one with God our Father (His prayer in *John* 17), reconciled and made fit companions and family members of a God who is holy love.

Atonement as At-onement

Associated with an understanding of real, experiential reconciliation is a fuller, Jesus-centered understanding of what atonement means. The etymology of the word atonement is a study in itself. As related to the concept of reconciliation, the word takes on a significance that has helped to uncover what restorative reconciliation is all about. Atonement is one of those words whose meaning has changed over time. Years ago, I simply accepted the meaning of atonement as *reparation for a wrong or an injury. To make amends*. I have discovered more about atonement since then.

At the time the King James Bible was written in 1611, the word *one* was both a pronoun and a verb. If two friends had parted ways through a breach of trust or a conflict, I might say "I am going to intervene and one them back into friendship." The underlying meaning was to bring back to unity, to oneness, to be at-one in a relationship. Atonement was the melding of at-one-ment and carried the sense of reconciliation.

However, over time the meaning of at-one changed, becoming the word *atone* and merging into the concept of reparation. When absorbed into theological understandings coming out of the penalty and satisfaction theories of the Middle Ages, the meaning of *atonement* was squarely aligned with the meaning of making-up-for. Jesus' sacrifice on the cross has been almost exclusively seen in theologies of the West through the lens of *covering*, making up for, making reparation. And Jesus is depicted as the substitute who makes reparation for us, in our place.

However, the main meaning of atonement in the Old Testament has to do with cleansing and purging, an existential reality that could not be fully achieved by sacrificing animals. Jesus chose to give His entire earthly life for us, including dying sacrificially for us. His was self-giving love, not ritualistic animal blood sprinkled on an altar. He shed His love through shedding His blood. His forgiving love cleansed us, as did His purging of human nature by sacrificially crucifying the old self. Real reconciliation could happen only when human nature was involved, not animal nature. And in Old Testament thinking, real reconciliation between God and mankind couldn't happen until Messiah came.

Well, again, Messiah came. Who could have guessed that in Himself, Jesus the Messiah would be "the Way, the Truth, and the Life," enabling humankind to re-enter a real reconciling union with God and with one another?

A foundational dimension of the mission of the Son of God was to bridge the gap sin had caused between a holy God and us. Through Jesus, and in Him, we are immersed into real reconciliation, restored to real relationship with God. We can have our hearts opened to the truth of God's character and our true identity. Jesus has *at-oned* us by restoring the existence on earth of a holy, loving human nature, one conformed to the image of God's own nature, and therefore one which is fit for fellowship with a holy God.

At-onement denotes the new world order of bringing God's love and way of life onto the earth. I think that we have barely scratched the surface of what it means to love and live in the way Jesus demonstrated: the death of the old life exchanged for His new, resurrected life. Jesus brought the Kingdom of God upon the earth. He now continues to spread its rule and reign through co-laboring with those who have immersed themselves into Him.

2000 years into the Christian Age, and we are only slowly growing into Jesus' victorious body here on earth. We are still far from daring to claim fully our identity in Him as sons and daughters of the Sovereign of the universe, who is also our Father. We are still slow in allowing Holy Spirit to make the kind of changes and exchanges in us that will advance the Kingdom of God. In the center of real repentance and spiritual revival is the humble acknowledgment that we are His, we belong to Him in a relational sense. He pursues us and invites us to return home, to take our place in His Kingdom, in His family. This is where we belong.

The Divine Exchange Transfusion

The following Scriptures and diagram are presented to express visually the dynamic flow of God's plan for the restoration of His creation. In the diagram on the next page, **Exchange** means that something is removed and replaced by something else. In the death of Christ Jesus, God flushes out the entirety of sin and evil: all behavior and the entire self-bent human heart. He also takes onto Himself all the wounds and sorrows from the impact of evil, and all the wrong ways we have devised to manage personal pain—defensiveness, denial, projection, etc.

In the resurrection, a new Man comes out of the tomb, stretching out His arms to welcome all who will receive His embrace and become His brothers and sisters. The first Adam is replaced by the second Adam. In Him we become second-Adam brothers and sisters.

The dynamic flow of God is also a kind of **Transfusion**. The false self, embedded in each of us, is like diseased blood. God allowed all wickedness to pour out upon Jesus so it could be crucified, disposed of, like the waste blood of a transfusion. Then, after the resurrection, the risen life of Jesus becomes a kind of *donor blood*: the life-filled "righteousness" of *2 Corinthians* 5:21. Believers become this righteousness as Holy Spirit replicates in them the same dynamic process that flowed through Jesus in His death and resurrection.

This replication began after Jesus returned to His Father in the Ascension and the power of Holy Spirit filled new believers at Pentecost (*Acts* 2:1-4). It is Scripturally clear that the mission of Holy Spirit is to impart the risen human nature of Jesus into the hearts of humankind. As we abide in Him, we become what He accomplished. In Jesus, God became like us so that we can become like Him (*2 Corinthians* 3:18; *1 John* 3:2; and *2 Peter* 1:4).

THE DIVINE EXCHANGE TRANSFUSION IN JESUS

"For He made Him who knew no sin to be sin for us, that we might become the righteousness of God in Him."
(2 Corinthians 5:21 NKJV)

"We know that our old self was crucified with him in order that the body of sin might be brought to nothing, so that we would no longer be enslaved to sin."
(Romans 6:6 ESV)

"... put on the new self, created to be like God in true righteousness and holiness."
(Ephesians 4:22-24 ESV)

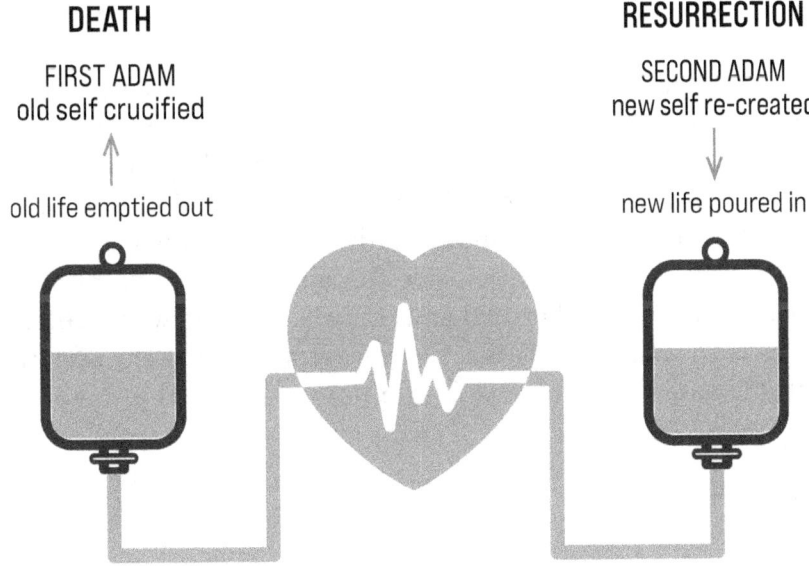

DEATH	RESURRECTION
FIRST ADAM	SECOND ADAM
old self crucified	new self re-created
old life emptied out	new life poured in

"... that he might be the firstborn among many brothers and sisters."
(Romans 8:29 NIV)

A heart transplant

Another evocative image to express what I believe to be at the core of God's invitation to us in the Gospel comes from the prophet Ezekiel. Ezekiel opened his creative heart to let Holy Spirit express some of the most vivid imagery recorded in the Bible. God speaks through him: "Moreover, I will give you a new heart and put a new spirit within you, and I will remove the heart of stone from your flesh and give you a heart of flesh. I will put My Spirit within you and cause you to walk in My statutes, and you will keep My ordinances and do them" (*Ezekiel* 36:26-27 AMP).

I submit that the heart of stone is the Adamic, stubborn, selfish, false self. That heart was fully *displaced* at the cross. Then this false self was totally *replaced* at the resurrection when Jesus (having been tested and found true) fully became that "heart of flesh" into which "My Spirit" could dwell. When God spoke through Ezekiel to Israel, He was speaking about what would first come through Messiah, then to the nation Israel, then to all people the world over.

Who could have imagined that this heart replacement would take place by the Son of God Himself, reaching down to us as *Savior* (in Hebrew, *the extended arm of Yahweh*), reaching into the darkened human heart so He could resist every temptation to seek self first? Who could have imagined that the Son of God would Himself come to earth so He could get inside our fallenness to perform a heart transplant. The surgical procedure is there for all who would come to Him to receive it, knowing that such a radical procedure is necessary ... that it was and is a matter of life or death. And God's plan was and is to give us life.

Coming home

Finally, I offer to you the story of the prodigal son (*Luke* 15), as a story that depicts God's heart, our journey, and the mission of Jesus. One of the most memorable verses in the Bible, and one that continues to touch my heart deeply, is verse 20: "And he [the prodigal] arose and came to his father. But when he was still a great way off, his father saw him and had compassion, and ran and fell on his neck and kissed him." Here we see the heart of our Father. He is poised and eager for all His children, near and far, to return to Him. His heart is that none would perish (*2 Peter* 3:9), but that all would turn from wherever they are in their own lost ways, and return to Him (In the Hebrew language, the word for *return* is the same as that used for *repent*.).

The Incarnation is about Jesus Christ entering and inhabiting fallen human existence so He can wake us up, bring humanity to its senses, and be the human being who "came to himself" (v.17). Not that He ever sinned. Rather, He entered our prodigal, lost, self-first fallenness and refused to be fallen in it. He resisted every temptation to sin, and in doing so He turned and returned human existence back towards Father God. "Follow Me home," He would encourage, "our Father awaits your arrival."

Jesus was gradually causing human nature (through His own human body and soul), to do what we couldn't do: He "came to himself. . . . And he arose and came to his father" (v.17). In what I consider to be the best Scriptural sense of the word, Jesus *substituted* for us, but not by taking our place and getting tortured and divinely whacked in the death-penalty box. Rather, in *solidarity*, He joined us in our place of lostness. He experienced our suffering, shame, rejection, and death so He could absorb it and replace it with His risen life. He took us off a path that was indeed leading to eternal death and set us on a path within Himself that not only leads to life, but is Life.

In other words, He entered our place of fallenness in order to replace all the sin and pain with His newly risen life, that He might lead us and enable us to find our way to our intended destination: back home with our Father. Jesus caused lost humanity to wake up and realize that we are lost and need to be found, that we are dead and cannot come alive by anything we do by our own striving.

Jesus brings us home. At the end of this beautiful story, the father joyfully proclaims to his eldest son: "It was right that we should make merry and be glad, for your brother was dead and is alive again, and was lost and is found" (v.32).

I believe that in this very moment, God our Father would say to each of us, "Arise, my son, my daughter, embrace My Son who is your

Lord, Redeemer, and Brother. He walks alongside you when you are lost and He beckons you even now to come home. Rise up in Him and with Him, and let Him accompany you home, where you belong. And when you return, know that even as you are still a great way off, I will see you, love you, run to you, fall on your neck, and kiss you. Come, my children, come home."

> Bring my sons from afar and my daughters from the end of the earth, Everyone who is called by my name, whom I created for My glory, Whom I formed and made (*Isaiah* 43:6-7 ESV).

DISCOVERY GEMS

The following is a summary of discovery gems garnered from the 14 years of this project.

◊ **Incarnation as Restoration.** From my earliest days, the image of God most dominant in how I viewed God was that of an easily offended monarch who was mostly concerned with what I was doing wrong. Following from this concept was His supposed focus on judgment and punishment. My image of God included the concept of Jesus as my death-penalty substitute.

For my view to be altered, it has taken many years of a process similar to a laser beam breaking up cataracts. Over the span of these past 14 years, my inquiries took me into the Incarnational-Trinitarian theology of the Eastern Orthodox Church. What has been like a healed lens is seeing God as a relational Being who desires my companionship. I no longer see Him as a mirthless monarch sitting on a throne with a scepter in one hand and a gavel in the other.

Broadening my view of God has greatly enhanced my sense of the thrust of the Incarnation. The propelling gesture that came into view was a triune God of relationships, stooping down in incomprehensible compassion and humility in the person of Jesus Christ, and scooping us up. In the first creation, God had breathed His very life into our nostrils, pouring into the deepest layers of our DNA His own likeness and character. In the second creation at the resurrection, God re-breathed His life into the second Adam, Jesus, so we could abide in Him and receive His life, thereby becoming His brothers and sisters.

The main Scripture stories that reveal the intentions of this God of relationships are: (a) The story of Hosea and Gomer—God pursuing us, wooing us, redeeming us off the slave block. The fulfillment of Hosea is Jesus. (b) The story of the *Song of Songs*, with Jesus as the fulfillment of the husband coming for us, desiring intimacy with us.

(c) The Bridegroom Jesus in the *Book of Revelation* returning to claim His bride.

◊ **Rescuing Us from the Miry Pit**. God's relentless pursuit of us, intending for us to have relational union with Him, led to a deeper understanding of the Incarnation as: *Rescuing*—we were lost; *Redeeming*—we were enslaved; *Reclaiming*—we were stolen by the devil; and *Reviving*—we were immersed in and drinking from a river of death. This contaminated water was a toxic brew of which arch-narcissist Satan was the master chef. Jesus came to pull us from this muddy river of death and detoxify human nature of the lethal poison that had permeated our bodies and souls.

Outside of living in Christ Jesus, we are caricatures of what God intended, mere shadows of His image and likeness. A pervasive darkness continues to settle into the cultures of our world, like a stealthy, creeping fog. It is now perhaps more imperative than ever to see that deep penetration into and transformation of human nature is the core mission of Jesus in the Incarnation. It is a mission motivated by God's intention to have us live with Him for all eternity as close companions. But we need to be radically altered, enlivened, and returned to our true selves—which the Son of God has accomplished in Himself and now dispenses to us through Holy Spirit.

Understanding the depth of Jesus' immersion into human nature through the Incarnation was an enliveningly rich excursion in my journey, especially during these past 6 years. Seeing Jesus' faithful decisions to resist every temptation during His lifetime, responding every time with truth and goodness, gave me a deeper appreciation for His extravagant commitment to God and to us.

It was deeply comforting to have confirmed how much God really wants us to be with Him as companions. Jesus gave His all so we could come home with Him. Truly He is a faithful shepherd, brother, and friend.

◊ **The End of Retributive Justice**. The most significant upheaval in my understanding of who God is came through much prayer and desiring to know more about the cross of Jesus. I listened carefully as Jesus spoke the words: "You have heard that it was said, 'an eye for an eye and a tooth for a tooth.' But I tell you not to resist an evil person .... You have heard that it was said, 'You shall love your neighbor and hate your enemy.' But I say to you, love your enemies, bless those who curse you ..." (*Matthew* 5:38-44). Jesus is the definitive revelation of what God wants to say to us. These words of His are weighty indeed.

As I asked Holy Spirit to take these words of *Matthew* 5 deep into my soul, I was able to write chapters 12, 13, and 14. Ironically, the retributive justice (an eye for an eye) heaped upon Jesus by the Pharisees, the Romans, and the fear-driven people was exactly the "justice" Jesus abolished in *Matthew* 5. It seems to me now that penal substitutionary atonement is a variation of this eye-for-an-eye principle, and I have dismissed this theory as Scripturally unviable.

In words and actions, Jesus Christ established and anchored the Kingdom of God on earth. On Good Friday, Jesus demonstrated what He had announced in *Matthew* 5 as the foundational Kingdom principle: unconditional, self-giving love, up to and including love for enemies. He had "poked some eyes" by speaking undiluted truth, and the offended parties "poked His eyes out" in commensurate retribution. What did He supposedly deserve for His "offenses"? The offended Pharisees and Romans decided that He deserved capital punishment laced with torture. And Jesus' response to these hateful enemies? "Forgive them, Father. . . ."

Those were the words that began the revolution that is Christianity. It is a revolution based on self-giving love, to the point of dying and forgiving, even in the most extreme circumstances of abuse and injury.

One personal piece of discovery about forgiveness was finding a place in my soul that held a remnant doubt about whether I had been fully forgiven for everything. Holy Spirit orchestrated an inner-healing session in me while I was writing Chapter 13. During the past few years, I have come to the realization that forgiveness, like God's compassion and mercy, is an intrinsic part of His loving heart. He doesn't need a ritual, a condition fulfilled, or a payment, in order to forgive. He simply wants us to turn to Him with repentant hearts. He forgives freely.

In imitation of our God, we are also to forgive freely. And we are to receive His forgiveness fully. I fully received God's forgiveness while writing my prayer in Chapter 13. I have released the residual ripples of anxiety that had been lurking in my old doubt about full forgiveness. Something feels cleaned out. A feeling of relief. Truth continues to set me free.

◊ **A Word about Warfare.** If Jesus abolished retribution and revenge as forces of overcoming evil, that is, if an "eye for an eye" is not the way of the New Covenant, does this nullify fighting or warfare when faced with evil? Jesus overcame evil with good, hate with love, enmity with forgiveness, darkness with light. He met force with force: He stood up to and resisted every temptation. In the swirl of intimidation and harassment, the Son of God steadfastly refused to be anything other than our Father's beloved and faithful Son. As such, He was teaching us how to fight.

Jesus' whole life on earth was war. He was continually accused and attacked. Going toe-to-toe with ruling forces of evil, in the face of a constant barrage of insults, threats, and lies, He countered with love and truth. He never once gave in to the ingrained inclination of humankind to look out for Himself first or to retaliate. His mission was to rescue us, and in every expenditure of energy He stayed true to laying down each moment of His life for our wellbeing. In addition to His other names, Jesus was and is our *Warrior King*. He is in charge of the war between the kingdom of darkness and the kingdom of God.

Through His enactment of holy love, Jesus triumphed. In Him the war has been won. Jesus said in *John* 16:33 that we would have affliction and trouble in this world, ". . . but be of good cheer, I have overcome the world." Within the person of the Son of God, a Man emerged from the sin-gnarled stock of Adam who was completely victorious over evil. And this Man invites us to dive into Him with our whole being. When we immerse ourselves by full-hearted faith into Him, allowing the Spirit to change us and facilitate exchanges in us, Jesus continues spreading His victory over evil, now through us. In Him, we can stand toe-to-toe with the hatred, harassment, and falseness that we encounter in our lives.

During the past 14 years of my journey, I have discovered more deeply my identity as a beloved son. However, in becoming more like Jesus, something has emerged to reveal that, like Jesus, I am to be a warrior. There is a war that Jesus has won in Himself, but the war is not finished here on earth where His body of believers exist: "Now you are the body of Christ and individually members of it" (*1 Corinthians* 12:27). There is yet much resistance to the kingdom of God by the enemy and his human pawns.

Victory comes for us the same way it came for Jesus: "not to be conformed to the world," and to say "no" to sin and "yes" to truth, self-giving, and goodness. Resisting the ways of the false self, combined with living in the truth and goodness of Jesus' life in us, constitute the true form of spiritual warfare.

An increased resolve has strengthened in me as I realize that the verse, "It is no longer I who live but Christ lives in me" (*Galatians* 2:20), means that I am a warrior, alongside and within my Warrior King. In Him I am called upon to advance the kingdom of God on earth by overcoming evil with good. As some of my warrior brothers in the Lord say, I am to be "dangerous" for accomplishing good. Believers are Jesus' band of brothers and sisters, bringing the reality of Jesus' redemption more and more onto the earth, as we allow Holy Spirit to continue restoring us.

◊ **Arise, My Sons and Daughters**. Another of my inquiries of the Lord was to clarify how Jesus' death and resurrection fit together. Slowly it came to me that the so-called "Finished Work" of Jesus is not finished at the cross as has been repeatedly asserted by theologians in the West for hundreds of years. The concept and diagram of what I call The Exchange Transfusion in Chapter 14 illustrate the two-phase approach of Paul, especially as articulated in *Romans* 6:6; *2 Corinthians* 5:21; and *Ephesians* 4:22-24.

In these passages, we can see Jesus' death as an emptying out old life, and His resurrection as the infilling of Holy Spirit into new life, as once again God breathed His life into the nostrils of a man (the Second Adam, Jesus). It is breathtaking to realize how radical and comprehensive The Great Exchange was and is.

The Finished Work of Jesus is His death and resurrection, and it was all done for us, to be a transformative process for us. In a real sense, the finishing of His work is now taking place on earth through His body of believers, as we become more and more like Him in each Christlike decision we make. The Incarnation continues, the Word becoming flesh, as He dwells more and more in us on earth. Perhaps this process of the Incarnation continuing through believers is a primary way these words are fulfilled: ". . . Your kingdom come, Your will be done, on earth as it is in heaven" (*Matthew* 6:10).

◊ **An Enhanced Understanding of the Lost Son Story.** I have often seen myself as the lost son, and in the first years of my real Christian walk I saw the elder son in me. Then, through maturity and growth in the Lord, the compassionate heart of the father found its way into my heart as well. And in the past four years, as intimacy with Jesus has grown, I now see Jesus in this parable in a surprisingly new way.

He entered fallen human existence in such a penetrating way that He stood in our shoes. He stood with us in the "miry pit," even down into the muck of the pigsty we live in, so He could lead us out. The lost son ". . . came to himself . . . . And he arose and came to his father" (*Luke* 15:17-20).

The strongest sense of Jesus as my *substitute* is right here in this part of the story. It is Jesus who has created the opportunity and possibility for humankind to come to our senses, to come to ourselves. In Him is this awakening, through the many steps He took in His human journey to resist sin, to say "no" to all evil ways. He accomplished perfection by suffering but never sinning (*Hebrews* 2:18). He did what no human being could do because all of us are helplessly lost in our own selfish ways: Jesus brought humanity back into God-designed human nature by standing in our human shoes and turning the direction of our feet back home.

He didn't act out the sinful ways of the lost son; instead, He turned away from every false, tempting step, and turned always to communion with His Father. And as we come alive in Him, as we eat and drink the perfect Son, we too can turn in the direction of home. Stuck in the self-centered squalor of our old selves, we can call out to

Jesus and "come to ourselves." He is our forerunner. We can wake up within the true-human consciousness of our brother, Jesus, and come home to our Dad, who is always ready and eager for our return.

This discovery is a reframing of the WWJD meme which asks: what would Jesus do? Rather than trying to imitate Jesus in our own strength, the reframe is to step by full faith into the turned-around steps Jesus has done in Himself. We stay in those footsteps by abiding in Him, like branches in the Vine, walking together, making the trek home to Dad. All God wants is for us to return to Him, and we can do that in and with Christ Jesus.

As I write these words, it seems as though this discovery of Jesus in the parable of the lost son may be the most precious of all my discovery gems during these past 14 years. A deeply comforting peace settles into my heart when I realize that the Incarnation Plan of God reveals His passionate and committed desire for me to live within God's triune fellowship. That is my true home. Equally precious is the realization that I make this journey home by living in and with the Lord Jesus Christ.

◊ **Discovery in a Painting**. Years ago, when looking through many images and paintings in search of a book cover for *Becoming the Likeness of Jesus*, I came upon a painting that riveted my attention. I contacted the artist and told him of my project, requesting permission to use his painting as my book cover. While talking with him, I learned that he had created the painting for his wife, giving it to her on their 25th wedding anniversary. Its title: *Two Hearts Beat as One*. This painting strikes me as perfect for this current book, and it is on the front cover.

I look at the painting and I see two hearts beating in unison because of the golden life-pulse that charges them both. I enter the painting and feel the life of Jesus coursing through and charging my heart with His vitality. I am shocked alive (regenerated) as a new creation, and given a new self in Christ Jesus, by the power of the Holy Spirit. "It is no longer I who live but Christ lives in me" (*Galatians* 2:20).

I know that this is the way I partake of divine nature (*2 Peter* 1:4). I know that I am not alone, and that Jesus will never leave me nor forsake me (*Hebrews* 13:5). And I am reminded of Jesus' picture of abiding in Him as a branch in a vine (*John* 15:4). The life-pulse of His heart charging and changing mine merges with an image of the sap enlivening a newly grafted branch. In Him I am made whole and fully alive.

Two Scriptures come to mind: "I will betroth you to Me forever; yes, I will betroth you to Me in righteousness and justice, in lovingkindness and mercy; I will betroth you to Me in faithfullness, and you shall know the Lord" (*Hosea* 2:19-20). "For your Maker is your husband" (*Isaiah* 54:5).

Astonishing and unfathomable though it seems, I firmly believe we are called into a relationship with Jesus that is a likeness of the two-becoming-one intimacy of marriage (*Genesis* 2:24). I look again at the book cover and see the two hearts made synchronous by the golden life-pulse. It is a *love-pulse*. I see God's ineffable love streaming out, heart to heart, wooing us into a relationship wherein He pulls us to Himself in a love embrace. There, in His embrace, He enlivens us, restores us, and makes us like Himself so we can be suitable companions with Him, and with one another, for all eternity.

I feel moved to end with an exhortation. After twenty centuries into the Christian era, a profound identity crisis still engulfs earth's inhabitants. Many remain in the dark about their true identity as children of God.

> *People must know that we all are God's children, whose destiny is to return home, and that Jesus is our brother who has come to bring us home, where we belong.*

RESOURCES

Chapter 2. Long Day's Journey into Night

· John Eldredge and Brent Curtis, *The Sacred Romance*. How men are wounded in childhood.

· Warren Smith, *The Light that was Dark*. The author spent several years within New Age spirituality and shares discoveries he made, especially about how the occult community handled the reality of evil.

Chapter 3. Dawn Breaks Through

· C.S. Lewis, *Mere Christianity*. God is Real and we become real persons in Jesus.

Chapter 5. Exchanges For Life: Jesus Exchange Ministry

· I recommend two Christian inner healing ministries: Transformation Prayer Ministry, transformationprayer.org; and Immanuel Prayer Ministry, immanuelprayerministry.com. Both ministries are based in the United States and have referral guides to trained facilitators in various cities and states. The ministry that I facilitate is a combination of TPM, Immanuel, and the Jesus Exchange protocol described in this chapter.

Chapter 6. God's Plan: Out with the Old, In with the New

· Earl Jabay, *The Kingdom of Self*.

· Oswald Chambers, *My Utmost for His Highest*. Several meditations in this tome focus on the old self's absorption with self-realization.

Chapter 7. Fixing Our Eyes Fully on Jesus

• Arthur Pink, *An Exposition of Hebrews*. Fixing our eyes on Jesus, the perfect image of God.

• C. Baxter Kruger, *Across All Worlds*. Also, *Jesus and the Undoing of Adam*. The author incorporates the thinking of the early Fathers of the Church into Western theology. Kruger's research from 20 years ago has been a major resource for my own discovery process, as can be seen especially in chapters 8-12 of *The Jesus Exchange*.

• Gustaf Aulen, *Christus Victor*. A thorough history and comparison of Eastern and Western theologies of the Incarnation.

• Hank Hanegraaff, *Truth Matters, Life Matters More*. The author describes many discoveries about God's intention for union with us, as described in Athanasius and other early Fathers of the Church.

Chapter 8. Rescuing Us from the Miry Pit

• N.T. Wright, *Simply Jesus*. Exegesis of how and why Jesus can be called the *New Exodus*.

Chapter 9. Reclaiming What Had Been Stolen

• Gustaf Aulen, *Christus Victor*. Tracks the threads of restorative theology in the early Church.

• John Crowder, *Cosmos Reborn*. History and approaches of restorative theology.

• Timothy Jennings, *The God-shaped Brain, and The God-shaped Heart*. Major resources for significant discoveries about penalty atonement; effects of the Fall; the Law of Love; sin as disease.

Chapter 10. The Divine Dilemma

· Bill Day, *Becoming the Likeness of Jesus*. From inner healing ministry to lifelong sanctification.

· C. Baxter Kruger, *Across All Worlds*. Delineates the divine dilemma.

· David Takle, *Lamb of God*. A thorough examination of penal substitution theory, offering in its place an Exchanged Life view of Atonement.

· Derek Flood, *Healing the Gospel*. Restorative theology. Re-examining why Jesus came.

· Gustaf Aulen, *Christus Victor*.

· N.T. Wright, *The Day the Revolution Began*. Cultural context and theology of Good Friday.

· Jennings, *The God-shaped Brain*. How the law of love operates.

Chapter 11. The Death of Sin and the Sin-prone Old Self

· Kruger, *Across All Worlds*. Also, *Jesus and the Undoing of Adam*.

· James Beilby (ed.), *The Nature of the Atonement*. Especially the Christus Victor model.

· Jennings, *The God-shaped Brain*.

· Jennings, *The Remedy New Testament*. (Expanded Paraphrase in Everyday English)

Chapter 12. A Whole Lot of Pouring Going On

· Derek Flood, *Healing the Gospel*.

· N.T. Wright, *The Day the Revolution Began*.

Chapter 13. A Tale of Two Facets

- Brian Zahnd, *Sinners in the Hands of a Loving God*. Jesus and the end of retributive justice

- David Takle, *Lamb of God*.

- Jennings, *The God-shaped Brain*. Also, *The God-shaped Heart*.

Chapter 14. Arise, My Son!

- C.S. Lewis, *Mere Christianity*.

- Crowder, *Cosmos Reborn*.

- Jennings. *The God-Shaped Brain*.

- Jonathan Cahn, *The Oracle*. Jesus returning as the Bridegroom.

DISCOVERY GEMS

- Michael Thompson, *King Me*. Restoring true masculinity. Jesus our Warrior King.

APPENDIX I

- Dallas Willard, *Hearing God*.

AFTERWORD

Through recent podcasts and writings, I have learned that at least two of the authors listed in RESOURCES and BIBLIOGRAPHY have modified their theological views since writing the books I have referenced. I do not endorse or ascribe to perspectives which seem to have veered into universalism. My intention in *The Jesus Exchange* is to bring a fresh re-statement of the Gospel, not to create a new gospel.

I have tried to express a truth that has mostly been hidden in the West for hundreds of years. This truth is about the dynamic transformation that takes place in those who choose to immerse themselves into a relationship with Jesus. In these darkened days, I believe it is time for more of God's light to flow through us into the world, from the deposit of truth and love that is in Christ Jesus. In *Matthew* 5:14-16, the Light of the world tells those who have plunged into Him, "You are the light of the world.... Let your light so shine before men...."

I have drawn from Western Christianity as embodied in the Nicene Creed and the Apostles' Creed. I have also delved into Eastern Christianity by expressing several perspectives from Eastern Orthodox theology. Hopefully, this blended understanding (West and East) of The Great Exchange is *orthodox* in a broader sense of the word: Scripturally grounded discovery in an ongoing pursuit of truth.

APPENDIX I

Interacting with God: Observations and Guidelines

In childhood and into adult years, I talked to God by asking for things, telling Him how majestic He was, asking for help, requesting protection from the wiles of the devil, and confessing sins. Throughout my Catholic years, I had a sense of living in two separate worlds—a *religious* world of prayer, Mass, and sacraments, and a *daily-life* world. God was in charge of the first world, I was in charge of the second, though I believed I needed His help to get through. As a seminarian and a theologian, I lived in a third world: a *mental* world filled with thoughts and doctrines about God.

In all three worlds, God-talk was plentiful, but God Himself seemed removed and remote. I didn't have any idea that I could just talk with God as though He were a person standing next to me. Even the thought of the Holy Spirit being within me seemed abstract and impersonal. The reciprocity implied in the word *interaction* was missing.

Absent in all those years was a simple, conversational context in which I might ask a question like, "Lord, what is your perspective on this situation?"—with an expectation that He would answer, and that I could listen and directly receive His answer.

Later, after my years in Humanism, as I slipped into a New Age spiritual mindset, God became an impersonal force that I believed could be felt or intuited in the right circumstances. Names such as Universal Consciousness, The Source, or The Universe were used to describe God, but such abstract concepts ruled out personal engagement.

Phrases such as "I thank the universe" or "I think the universe is telling me to change careers" were typical expressions I heard and repeated, but there was no personal dimension in which to have dialogue or interaction. Similar to my Catholic days, it never dawned on me that personal engagement with God was possible.

In 1984, at age 42, God initiated interaction by speaking "I am Life," and I responded by pulling the plug on my many pseudo life-supports. Several years later, I sat at a kitchen table, a Bible open in front of me, and directly asked God to show me whether or not this book was His inspired Word. As I read some passages, the words came alive. Someone alive was speaking the verses. My question was being answered personally: This book called the Bible was indeed His Word. This marked the beginning of conversational prayer with God, but more years would go by before a flow of conversation became normal and regular.

In the first years after 2000, the process of Jesus-centered inner healing opened up new dimensions in experiencing how much God desires to engage with us personally. All healing sessions that I facilitated or received took place within the context of dialogues with Him. His personal presence becomes more and more real as I have continued to facilitate Jesus Exchange sessions.

However, I have observed that there is a mindset in many churches that believes God spoke through the writers of the Bible and then stopped speaking. This thinking views the Word of God as totally contained and captured in the pages of a book. It is similar to the doctrine of the Sadducees in Jesus' time, which taught that God stopped speaking after He finished speaking with Moses.

Let me be clear, I believe that the Bible is the inspired written Word of God. It is a written record of the saving truth spoken by God, and reliably sets the boundaries and parameters of what He has to say to humankind. But the Word of God is not just the Bible. The Bible is not Jesus Christ who is the living Word of God. Jesus Himself said to these Sadducees, "You search the Scriptures because you think that in them you have eternal life; it is these that bear witness of Me; and you are unwilling to come to Me so that you may have life" (*John* 5:39-40). The Bible points to Jesus as a personal fount of real life.

The wooden thinking that views the Word of God as totally *contained* inside the pages of a book cannot conceive of the spiritual reality of God *continuing to speak*. For many of my first 42 years I embraced this wooden thinking, but now I know for myself that God does not intend the Bible to be a static receptacle, a repository to be intellectually accessed and then stored in my mind, like a reference book in a library.

I have thought of the Bible as though it were a user's manual for a car, to learn the way God wants my life to operate, then to apply the directions I find in the manual. But now I know that God speaks to me, Person to person, through the power of the Holy Spirit. When I read Scripture, I first anchor myself by prayer into the presence of Holy Spirit. I become aware of my relationship with the Lord, and I begin to listen to Him and wait for Him to speak to me on this day, in this moment, as I enter into dialogue with Him.

Sometimes He speaks to me through the written words of the Bible, and sometimes He speaks to me in words that are not direct quotes from the Bible but are in accord with the written Word. His is a *living Word*, not just because it is lively, meaningful, and rich in content. His Word is a living Word because *He is still speaking*. It is not a past tense, done deal. He wants to continue speaking with whomever listens, and I have finally begun to listen.

The Word of God was still speaking when Jesus made a personal connection with my patient, Nancy, via an image of Himself and words of love (Chapter 1). Perfect love was casting out fear (*1 John* 4:18). When Jesus told me I was no longer a slave but a son, God was still speaking the words of *Galatians* 4:7, now to me, in the present moment.

There is still a lot of religious fog hiding the relational reality of God and hiding the continuous acts of God in any moment. I believe the following: He is still breathing His life into us, making us living souls (*Genesis* 2:7); we live and move and have our being in Him (*Acts* 17:28); He speaks through the marvelous natural world of His creation (*Psalms* 19); He speaks through images, pictures, and parables; He speaks in the circumstances of our lives; He speaks directly to us in conversation; and He speaks as we worship Him individually and corporately. He has never stopped speaking since the beginning: "In the beginning was the Word..." (*John* 1:1). The question is, *will we listen and respond?*

I believe God would have us reach out in faith to meet Him, to interact with Him. He wants to talk with us in two-way conversations. I feel His eagerness to do so.[9]

Dangerous waters

Yes, the potential for danger lurks in encouraging people to hear from God and to experience Him directly. People can go off the deep end. "Voices" can be one's own inner self-talk, auditory and visual hallucinations from pathologically disturbed minds, or demonic voices that come to us through ungodly thoughts and perceptions.

As whole denominations and churches have plunged into mysticism and wildly charismatic streams, a shudder runs through us when we hear the words, "God told me." Abject foolishness and devastating tragedy have followed in the wake of those words—witness the utterances of defunct American cult leaders, Jim Jones and David Koresh. There are counterfeits, fakery, and confusion. Keen discernment is needed now more than ever.

However, there is another danger: going off the *shallow* end. This is a more "respectable" danger, but as devastating and distorting as the deep end. One day Jesus walked into a synagogue and healed a blind man on the Sabbath. The Jewish leaders, proud of being Moses' disciples, "knew" that Jesus could not possibly be God because working on the Sabbath was clearly not allowed. They "knew" the Scriptures, and Jesus was clearly a sinner.

Even when confronted by the healed blind man, who said "One thing I do know, that though I was blind, now I see" (*John* 9:25), the Pharisees rejected the work because it did not conform to their legalistic ideas. They said, "We know that God has spoken to Moses, but as for this man, we do not know where He comes from" (v. 29). They did not know the living God in His love and mercy, even though He was

---

[9] For anyone who wants guidance for conversing with God, I recommend Mark Virkler: cwgministries.org and David Takle: kingdomformation.org. On their websites you will find Biblical documentation and practical guidelines for a conversational relationship with God.

standing there in front of them.

With the same legalistic fervor, many denominations react to "charismania" (extreme variations of the Charismatic Movement) by shutting down the possibility of hearing from God and experiencing Him in personal interactions. Of course we must be wary, but there is no Scriptural evidence for the total denial of hearing from God. Quite the contrary.

Examples abound in Scripture of personally interacting with the Lord:

In the Old Testament, (1) There is the amazing passage in *1 Samuel* 3:9-10 in which Samuel says, "Speak, Lord, for your servant is listening." And after this passage, Samuel's life of having two-way conversations with God unfolds. (2) Moses dialogued with God as two friends might talk (*Exodus* 33:11, for example).

In the New Testament, (3) Jesus daily devoted time to converse with His Father. The conversations were not one-way prayer speeches; He was in dialogue with His Father: "... for all things that I have heard from My Father I have made known to you" (*John* 15:15). And then He prays in *John* 17:3 "that they may know You, the only true God, and Jesus Christ whom You have sent." It is a prayer toward us having the same interaction with the Father that He does. Also, in *John* 16:13-15, Jesus tells us clearly that the Holy Spirit will be coming and "will guide you into all truth," and that "whatever He hears He will speak.... He will take of Mine and declare it to you." (4) In Paul's conversations with the Lord, three times he begged Him to remove the famous "thorn in the flesh." God was not silent. He responded and said, "My grace is sufficient for you, for My strength is made perfect in weakness" (*2 Corinthians* 12:9). How did God speak to Paul: In an audible voice? By the "still small voice" (*1 Kings* 19:12)? Or did God join His thought to Paul's receptive thinking, and the two thoughts became one in Paul's mind? I don't know, but whatever the case, Paul directly pleaded before the Lord, and the Lord responded.

What I have discovered in my interactions with God

Back in 1984, in Brightmoor Tabernacle, when I heard the words

"I am life," I felt hope, but I was wary. As far as I knew then, this was just the next adventure of my ongoing explorations looking for truth and healing. Deciding to immerse myself in the experience, my intention was to discover whether this "life" was real and to know whether the person who spoke was real.

The title of Chapter 4 is *A New Day*. I mean the word "Day" to refer to my last name as well as to indicate a sense of newness that came upon me when the Lord spoke the words, "You are no longer a slave but My son." The chasm of separation from my decades-long attachment disorder was filled with the substance of *belonging, relational attachment*, and *identity*. Similar to the centurion's servant in *Matthew* 8:9, Jesus spoke the word and I was healed. For many years I had pursued people, knowledge, drugs, and therapies of many varieties. However, the separation and pain had always remained. I can't adequately describe the healing that has settled into my soul through the sense of *belonging in my true family of origin in the Kingdom of God*, but it feels as though I am moving through a transition similar to that of going from a caterpillar to a butterfly.

In Chapter 5, I recounted the inner-healing experience I received in which the deeply buried cancerous lie that *God had rejected me* was expunged from my soul with one swift stroke from the Surgeon's scalpel. The truth of God's love and purposes for me poured in to close the wound and replace a sense of *rejection* with an awesome, overwhelming balm of *acceptance*. Over previous decades, I had gone to extreme measures to deal with this rejection wound. Nothing worked until my soul surgery.

It is now 30 years since the time of these healings. From my heart I can say the words in the *Book of Zephaniah* 3:17: "The Lord has calmed and quieted me with His love." As I write these words, I feel His Love, I feel His Presence, I feel His Peace.

BIBLIOGRAPHY

Athanasius of Alexandria. *On the Incarnation*. Columbia, SC: Pantianos Classics, 2020.
Aulen, Gustaf. *Christus Victor*. Eugene, OR: Wipf & Stock, 2003.
Beilby, James (ed.). *The Nature of the Atonement*. Downers Grove, IL: IVP Academic, 2006.
Bromiley, G.W. (ed.). *The International Standard Bible Encyclopedia*. Grand Rapids, MI: Wm. B. Eerdmans Publishing, 1979.
Cahn, Jonathan. *The Oracle*. Lake Mary, FL: Charisma Media, 2019.
Chambers, Oswald. *My Utmost for His Highest*. Grand Rapids, MI: Discovery House, 1992.
Crowder, John. *Cosmos Reborn*. Portland, OR: Sons of Thunder, 2013.
Dalbey, Gordon. *Healing the Masculine Soul*. Dallas: Word Publishing, 1988.
Day, Bill. *Becoming the Likeness of Jesus*. Buffalo, MN: Pyramid Publishers, 2018.
Day, William. *Healing Troubled Hearts*. Buffalo, MN: Pyramid Publishers, 2014.
Eldredge, John, and Brent Curtis. *The Sacred Romance*. Nashville, TN: Thomas Nelson, 1997.
Flood, Derek. *Healing the Gospel*. Eugene, OR: Cascade Books, 2012.
Frangipane, Francis. *The Power of One Christlike Life*. Cedar Rapids, IA: Arrow Publications, 2011.
Guyon, Jeanne. *Experiencing the Depths of Jesus Christ*. Sargent, GA: Christian Books Publishing House, 1975.
Hanegraaff, Hank. *Truth Matters, Life Matters More*. Nashville, TN: Thomas Nelson, 2019.
Huegel, F.J. *Bone of His Bone*. Fort Washington, PA: CLC Publications, 2009.

Jabay, Earl. *The Kingdom of Self*. Plainfield, NJ: Logos International, 1974.

Jennings, Timothy. *The God-shaped Brain*. Downers Grove, IL: Intervarsity Press, 2017.

Jennings, Timothy. *The God-shaped Heart*. Grand Rapids, MI: Baker Books, 2017.

Jennings, Timothy. *The Remedy*. Chattanooga, TN: Lennox Publishing, 2016.

Jeremiah, David. *Ten Questions Christians are Asking*. San Diego, CA: Turning Point, 2015.

Jones, Peter. *One or Two: Seeing a World of Difference*. Escondido, CA: Main Entry Editions, 2010.

Kraft, Charles H. *Deep Wounds, Deep Healing*. Ventura, CA: Regal Books, 1993.

Kruger, C. Baxter. *Across All Worlds*. Jackson, MS: Perichoresis Press, 2007.

Kruger, C. Baxter. *Jesus and the Undoing of Adam*. Jackson, MS: Perichoresis Press, 2003.

Kurath, Edward. *I Will Give You Rest*. Post Falls, ID: Divinely Designed, 2003.

Kylstra, Chester and Betsy. *Restoring the Foundations*. Santa Rosa Beach, FL: Proclaiming His Word, 2001.

Lehman, Karl. *The Immanuel Approach*. Evanston, IL: Immanuel Publishing, 2016.

Lewis, C.S. *Mere Christianity*. Riverside, NJ: Macmillan Publishing, 1952.

Lyons, Eric and Thompson, Bert. *In the Image and Likeness of God*. Montgomery, AL: Apologetics Press, 2002.

McGrath, Johanna and Alister. *Self-Esteem: the Cross and Christian Confidence*. Wheaton, IL: Crossway Books, 2002.

Mitchell, Timothy (ed.). *The Original Aramaic New Testament in Plain English*. New South Wales, Australia: Lulu Publishing, 2012.

Murray, Andrew. *Abide in Christ*. New Kensington, PA: Whitaker House, 1979.

Murray, Andrew. *The True Vine*. Chicago: Moody Publishers, 2007.

Murray, John. *Redemption Accomplished and Applied*. Grand Rapids, MI: Eerdmans Publishing, 1955.
Nee, Watchman. *The Spiritual Man*. New York: Christian Fellowship publishers, 1977.
Nouwen, Henri. *The Return of the Prodigal Son*. New York: Doubleday, 1992.
Paxson, Ruth. *Life on the Highest Plane*. Chicago: Moody Press, 1942.
Payne, Leanne. *Restoring the Christian Soul*. Grand Rapids, MI: Baker Books, 1991.
Penn-Lewis, Jessie. *Life in the Spirit*. Fort Washington, PA: CLC Publications, 1991.
Pink, Arthur. *An Exposition of Hebrews*. Grand Rapids, MI: Baker Book House, 1954.
Seamands, David A. *Healing Your Heart of Painful Emotions*. New York: Inspirational Press, 1993.
Smith, Ed M., and Smith, Joshua A. *The Essentials of Transformation Prayer Ministry*. Simpsonville, SC: New Creation Publishing, 2019.
Smith, Warren. *The Light that Was Dark*. Magalia, CA: Mountain Stream Press, 2005.
Takle, David. *Lamb of God*. High Point, NC: Kingdom Formation, 2018.
Takle, David. *The Truth About Lies and Lies About Truth*. High Point, NC: Kingdom Formation, 2016.
Tapscott, Betty. *Inner Healing Through Healing of Memories*. Kingwood, TX: Hunter Publishing, 1975.
The Original Aramaic New Testament in Plain English. New South Wales, Australia: Lulu Publishing, 2007.
Thompson, Curt. *Anatomy of the Soul*. Carol Stream, IL: Tyndale House, 2010.
Thompson, Michael. *King Me*. Columbia, SC: Zoweh, 2023.
Virkler, Mark and Patti. *4 Keys to Hearing God's Voice*. Shippensburg, PA: Destiny Image Publishers, 2010.
Willard, Dallas. *Hearing God*. Downers Grove, IL: Intervarsity Press, 1999.

Wright, N.T. *Simply Jesus*. New York, NY: Harper Collins, 2011.
Wright, N.T. *The Day the Revolution Began*. New York, NY: Harper Collins, 2018.
Zahnd, Brian. *Sinners in the Hands of a Loving God*. Colorado Springs, CO: Waterbrook, 2017.

SPIRITUAL REVIVAL IS UPON US

"In our current culture, we hear much about *sustainability*, and I've often wondered about that term as it applies to our spiritual lives, i.e., why haven't previous Christian revivals and movements taken hold and been sustainable? The answer to that question is clearly presented in *The Jesus Exchange*: Those previous revivals and movements focused on the individual's salvation (the "ticket" to eternal life) with very little attention focused on what happens after a person accepts Jesus as savior.

Numerous current-day prophets are confident that a huge world-wide revival is coming upon us, and *The Jesus Exchange* is perfectly timed to positively impact the harvest of souls ushered in by thousands and millions responding to this powerful move of the Holy Spirit. Within the pages of this book, we see the Scripture-based process of going from a believer to a personally transformed disciple. Everyone who wants to be engaged in real disciple-making should read this book!"

—Dr. Jeff Jeffries, president, Paradigm Consulting Services, Inc.

"What I love so much about *The Jesus Exchange* is the wonderful and clear explanation of what actually took place at the cross of Jesus Christ. Dr. Day explains that forgiveness most certainly was given when Jesus died on the cross, but that is not the complete story. Jesus' life, death, and resurrection also made possible our transformation and restoration back to God's original design. It opened wide the door to make right what had gone terribly wrong. I now have been given a much broader understanding of what Jesus provided for all of humanity. It makes my heart smile."

—Thomas Benner, men's ministry conference speaker, entrepreneur

www.ingramcontent.com/pod-product-compliance
Lightning Source LLC
Chambersburg PA
CBHW072208070526
44585CB00015B/1248